Bread and Freedom

Understanding and acting on human rights

Ron O'Grady

World Council of Churches
150 route de Ferney, 1211 Geneva 20, Switzerland

ACKNOWLEDGMENTS
The author gratefully acknowledges the assistance of Dr Jim Vietch,
lecturer in religious studies at Victoria University, Wellington, New
Zealand, for his comments on the writing of some chapters of this
book which were presented as a thesis for the South East Asia Graduate
School of Theology. Thanks also to Alison O'Grady for her invaluable
help in typing the manuscript for publication.

ISBN No. 2-8254-0594-9
Cover: An illustration by the imprisoned Filipino priest, Fr Ed de la
Torre, whose story is shared on page 32. The original painting was
done in prison and smuggled out to the Christian Conference of Asia
assembly in Penang, 1977, to illustrate the idea of "suffering and hope".
Under the right arm of Jesus people in subjection work under their
rulers on top of the pyramid. Under his left arm, people are depicted
rising up to their own dignity.
© 1979 World Council of Churches
No. 4 in the Risk book series

Table of contents

"We need to maintain both civil liberty and social justice as inseparable parts of human rights. As we cannot divide spirit and flesh in our body, so freedom and bread are integral to each other. If we lose one, we will distort all."

Statement of Indian Christians
from the consultation on
"The Indian Experience During Emergency"
held at Cochin, India, 24-31 August 1977

Introduction

The young man was explaining about his months in prison. He gave a terrible account of interrogation and torture and then added: "Of course there are many worse stories which I still cannot bring myself to repeat." He was in his early twenties, not long married and only out of prison for one week.

He explained the Christian commitment which had led him to give up a comfortable career in the city to work with the peasants, a job which had led to conflicts with the authorities, imprisonment and torture. Now on his release from prison he planned to return to the rural area.

"But isn't that dangerous?" I ask. He shrugs. "Possibly. Yes, I suppose it is."

I went to my home country and soon after heard the sequel. He had returned to work with the peasants, and just a few days after his arrival was standing beside the paddy field talking with some friends. Absorbed in their conversation, they didn't notice an unmarked car slowing to stop. From the car a man in civilian clothes pointed the automatic rifle and shot my young friend dead. The car sped off before the stunned villagers could react.

In that brief instant the blood of yet another un-named and little-known martyr had returned to the soil. His Christian obedience had meant death.

This particular incident took place in Asia. It could equally well have occurred in Latin America or Africa, for we are living in a time of history when repressive, centralized and technocratic governments have become common in many developing nations. In such nations, those Christians who choose to identify with the suffering and oppressed must expect to be in conflict with powerful political, economic and military interests if they attempt to take concrete action.

But the young man who died in the paddy field is not just a statistic or an abstract idea. To me, he is a face and a name and a voice. He is my encounter with redeeming love. He is my judgment.

It is by the witness of such young men that Christians throughout the *oikoumene* are being forced to probe the meaning of the worldwide struggle for human rights. In Asia this has become one of the priorities for the churches. In almost every Asian nation, a section of the church is asking new questions about human rights in relation to the government and to persons of other faiths.

In this book I am attempting to give some background to the debate as it takes place in Asia today. At the heart of the search are those events of recent history in which Christians have taken risks and suffered for their stand. It is from such living witness that we must try to trace our theological understanding of the events and to see what happens from a new perspective.

In my work, I am an ecumenical bureaucrat — a much maligned occupation, but one which has, I would affirm, an integrity in certain situations. The struggle for human rights is one of these. When we ask, which are the groups in Asia that take the ecumenical movement seriously, we have to answer that it is those on the frontiers, which struggle for the rights of the people but which do so from a lonely and vulnerable position. These witnesses to Christianity in the midst of social upheaval need the insights and encouragement of similar groups in other countries because their stand goes beyond nationalism to those deeper human realities of sin and suffering.

In the end, it is the victims of human rights violations who speak to us most poignantly of our own human condition. It was the victim on the cross who made us fully human through his suffering and death. Each subsequent victim becomes another sign of hope to the people. When all our words and reflections have been forgotten, their lives will continue to speak.

RON O'GRADY

Singapore
December 1978

I. Understanding the notion of human rights

Over the past two hundred years, the concept of "human rights" has proved to be one of the most enduring and creative catalysts for the social hopes of the people. It inspired those who formulated the great declarations of the French and American revolutions; it encouraged the reformers in their fight against slavery and torture; it was the foundation for declarations of the League of Nations and the United Nations; it was used to challenge the people during two world wars; and it has given hope to multitudes of oppressed communities.

Today it remains a powerful symbol of political, moral and economic and social aspirations. Whether from the American Senate in Washington or from a prison cell in Chile, seldom a day passes without some reference to human rights in the news media of the world. Few phrases have such moral weight and carry such universal conviction in the modern world.

Like all popular slogans, the concept of human rights is used indiscriminately. In the United States the gun lobby will invoke the right of every individual to carry a gun, and in Sweden it is argued that it is the right of every aged person to have a pension which would represent a fortune in developing nations. Neither of these could be termed "human rights", and we should therefore begin by distinguishing human rights from three similar but different concepts, namely civil, political and socio-economic rights.*

---

* (1) *Civil rights* is a more restrictive term which is related to a person's citizenship. Civil rights belong to a person or group because of the laws of the nation, and they are enforced through the "rule of law". Civil rights can be a powerful lever for the oppressed since they can be argued in a court of law, but since laws are easily changed by the government the people can also be victims of unjust laws and lose their civil rights. (2) *Political rights* are the rights of the people to participate in the variety of political processes. Although all political systems speak of political freedom, usually expressed through the ballot box, no society has fully succeeded in enabling the whole population to participate in the political process. With the complexity of modern society this would be impossible. There can only be degrees of political rights. (3) *Socio-economic rights* cover basic areas of food, shelter, health care and education. Again these are relative terms and are culturally and socially determined. The benefits of a welfare state are an example of socio-economic rights which are not universally enjoyed.

Human rights has a greater universality than these three. Human rights are those things which a person (or persons) can have a just claim to because of being a person. This is close to the intention of Jacques Maritain, the French philosopher, who spoke of "things which are owed to a man because of the fact that he is a man".[1]

Our concern, therefore, is with those rights which belong to all people, everywhere, at all times. When we say "the right to eat is a human right", we are speaking of something which is universally and morally true and which allows no exception. If a government or unjust economic system prevents the people from receiving food, then we are affirming that the people have a right to demand the food and, if all else fails, may even take it by force. This is the meaning of a human right. It belongs to the people.

Once we begin to explore the philosophy of the meaning of rights, we are driven back to religious convictions. There appears to be in the collective unconscious of the people a belief that there is a higher law than the laws given by kings and princes, law courts and governments. Such a belief is intrinsic in every religion and in Christianity is summarized in the affirmation of Peter that "obedience to God comes before obedience to man" (Acts 5 : 29).

This is not a book of philosophy so we are not required to go through the labyrinthian maze of definitions and counter-definitions in our concepts of freedom and rights. However, in order to give the parameters of the discussion we will summarize five affirmations about human rights on which the following text will be based.

1. Human rights must be understood in terms of relationships. Rights define the proper relationship between an individual and his/her community or between a group of people and their community.

Rights are not an individual matter applying only to one person or group of persons in isolation. They must be seen in relation to the whole community. At the same time the whole community relates to the rights of the individual. In the words of Gandhi "those who do not believe in the liberty of the individual believe in their own... if the individual ceases to count, what is left of society?" [2] We are thus requiring a balance in the relationship between extreme individualism and extreme communalism.

2. To affirm human rights is to assert human duties.

One cannot speak of human rights without the direct implication that society has a duty to uphold rights. If freedom of speech is a right, then society has a duty to protect the rights of its citizens to free speech.

Conversely, duties which are universally accepted give us an understanding of human rights. It is in this sense that the Bible speaks of human rights. The biblical commands imply rights. The commandment "Thou shalt not kill" implies the right not to be killed or, to put it positively, the right to life. The commandment not to steal implies property rights. There is a reciprocity of rights and duties.

3. It is a responsibility of human society to create those conditions of living in which human rights are protected. This includes action at the international, national and local level to encourage the establishment of institutions and the inculcation of attitudes which will ensure this protection.

Institutions exist to serve the people and not for their own sake. Yet each institution carries the seeds of corruption within it and must be constantly tested by the willingness of the institution to lay itself open to the people and to create structures of growth and freedom.

4. Gross violation of the rights of any individual or group is, by inference, a violation of the rights of all people.

To ignore or to condone individual actions which violate human rights is to invite a situation in which dehumanizing events can escalate and destroy a whole society. A threat to a part of the human race is an inherent threat to the whole.

5. Human rights are one and indivisible.

In the end there is only one right, the right to be human. Many economically poorer countries have begun to balance out some rights against others as a means of imposing a restrictive rule, and we must protest at this dehumanizing of the people. To offer bread without freedom or freedom without bread are both equally a denial of the rights of the people.

NOTES

1 Jacques Maritain: "The Rights of Man." In Maurice Cranston: *What Are Human Rights?* London: Bodley Head, 1973, p. 7.
2 Quoted by C. D. S. Devanesan and M. Abel: "The Powers of Government and the Claims of Human Freedom." In *Responsible Government in a Revolutionary Age*, ed. Z. K. Mathews. New York: Association Press, 1966, p. 209.

II. Historical context of the concern for human rights

The notion of rights has been a sustaining force for the people, but it has only been discovered by the masses in the last two hundred years. Prior to that time the concentration of power in the hands of a political elite was the dominant reality in western civilization. The feudal kings, lords, barons, bishops and tsars held the might and the people were subject to the caprice and patronage of their masters. Under a benevolent leader the conditions of the people might improve, but always they were subject to a rule of whim which denied any individual rights. In the closely-defined social structure, rights were accorded only to privileged groups. The Roman Empire had *salus populi* as its supreme law — the safety of the Roman people as a whole.[1] But this did not deter the emperors from sending Christians and other minority groups to the lions.

From the 11th century onwards wars of freedom played an increasing part in Europe's development. Although these were people's movements, the freedom sought was religious freedom rather than freedom for the people [2] and it did nothing to challenge the feudal structure of society. With the forced signing of the Magna Carta at Runnymede, England in 1215, new possibilities emerged. The barons' unrest was channelled into a demand that King John should make a solemn grant of liberties to the people. The critical clause 39 reads: "No freeman shall be taken or imprisoned... or exiled or in any way destroyed... except by the lawful judgment of his peers or (and) the law of the land."[3] Under the baronial system this was not as unconditional as the language would suggest. The Magna Carta "is in fact anything but democratic. Insofar as the 'people' figure in it at all, they figure as property."[4] The signing of the document was largely to protect the selfish interests of the barons and the church, and was not meant to assert rights and liberties for all.

Even so, it is still true that from the 13th century onwards the Magna Carta became an encouragement to people's movements throughout Europe. The establishment of the rule of law as superior even to the rule of kings and barons was a foundation stone of the search for the people's universal rights.

The search for rights in Asian cultures followed different routes. In Chinese society the place of the people had never been questioned by the philosophers. At the dawn of civilization in the reign of Shun (B.C. 2255-2198) the minister Kao-yao said: "Heaven hears and sees through (the eyes and ears of) our people. Heaven expresses its disapproval through the expressed disapproval of our people."[5] This gave rise to the traditional saying that "the will or heart of the people is the will of heaven. 民心天心 " Mencius develops the theme further in his *Book of History*: "The people are the most important, the spirits of the state the second, and the ruler the least important of all."[6] He also developed the theory of the equality of all people: "All men can be Tao and Shun (ideal Sage Emperors)."[7]

The ideal society would enable people to reach their goals: good life on earth, virtuous conduct, happiness and long life. In the perfect moral life, government and law would not be necessary.[8] These benevolent concepts from Confucius and Mencius were never actualized, but every ruler paid lip service to them, because only in this way could he retain "the mandate of heaven" under which he ruled.

Unlike the West, China possessed a single written language and a relatively homogeneous people. This gave a continuity in history and government which has built into its system protections for the rights of the people. Even so, many people were still exploited and consequently the same awakening to freedom which characterized western civilization was felt in China in the 19th century. Wars against the West and the hated Manchu rulers reached their climax with the T'aip'ing rebellion (called by contemporary Chinese a "revolution"),[9] a genuine people's movement which swept the whole of central China in the years 1850-1864. Ostensibly a religious movement, it actually gained its support from a confluence of several themes, including anger at oppressive rule, the desire for land reform, the decay of traditional religions and the gap between the wealthy and poor regions of China.[10] An attempt at socialist reform by the leaders was enlightened but failed, partly through lack of administrative experience.

In theory, China was a classless society, although in practice there were clear social distinctions. India, on the other hand, developed a society which was class-structured both in theory and in practice. The rights of the people were determined by the caste into which they were born. The caste system was reinforced by strong religious regulations, and this meant that any change in the system could come only from a religious movement. In ancient and medieval India many people's protest movements emerged from a religious base. Bhakti, or devotional movements, led by people like Ramanada and Kabir, attacked Brahmin supremacy and replaced Sanskrit texts with the vernacular, thus enabling the people to participate in worship. Buddhism also made a frontal attack on the Brahmins, and Sikhism began as a protest movement. Veerasaivism in the 12th century was an attack on the caste system.[11]

The caste system enabled people at least to have the class rights of their caste. Yet such is the diffuse nature of the Indian subcontinent and so strong the caste system that there was not the unity to stage a wide-based people's movement until the struggle for political independence in the 20th century.

From the 17th to the 20th century, in China and India as in almost every developing nation of Asia, Africa and Latin America, the people were the subjects of colonial rule, and although there were places and times where this influence was benign and benevolent, it did not provide the setting in which the people could find their full dignity and human worth. At the time when revolutionary people's movements in Europe were speaking of the rights of man and of citizens, rights were being denied to those under colonial rule.

The liberal revolutions

The latter part of the 18th century was a watershed period in the western history of human rights. In every part of Europe the vestiges of feudal society were dying and the people were discovering a new sense of their dignity. They began to discern that the pattern of society could be radically altered if egalitarian concepts were adopted and if the power of autocratic rule could be overthrown. The series of revolutions and social upheavals of that period were determinative in developing all subsequent western democratic philosophy and political life.

A new understanding of man had been articulated by a wide range of writers from the 17th century onwards. Philosophers and politicians such as John Locke, Adam Smith and John Stuart Mill in England; Voltaire, Diderot and Rousseau in France; Goethe and Kant in Germany; Benjamin Franklin and Thomas Paine in America, argued the meaning of freedom, and especially what it meant to be a free man in society. They believed that the universe was governed by natural laws which were capable of scientific and logical analysis; that man's reason could lead towards truth; that man could only develop his reason in freedom; that religion did not deprive man of his reason; and that society and government should work to preserve the natural laws and the natural rights of man.[12] At the heart of these concepts was the dimly understood perception that the people had entered politics as a force in their own right, and that they would no longer remain the pawns of a feudal power structure. This revolutionary idea opened up a new range of possibilities for changing the nature and structure of the political process.

By the 18th century the liberal ideas had become a significant political force. The bourgeoisie of "property and intelligence" which was emerging formed a base of people who had begun to see themselves as individuals rather than the property of a king or manor lord. A new educated class began to find a personal dignity which could be developed and even legally protected from the incursions of a ruling elite, and they sought for ways to introduce legal instruments for their own protection.

Today, when nationhood and the rights for national self-determination are accepted axioms, it is difficult to think back into a period when the people did not conceive of the nation as a political entity. The idea that the nation could be independent was a subversive doctrine in an age when tsars and emperors dominated their subject people. Political ideology was in its infancy, and even the leaders of the revolutions were motivated more by force of circumstance than by any ideological conviction. Both George Washington in 1775 and Maximillian Robespierre in 1789 were still monarchists but found themselves in a position where the forces of the people carried them forward to develop a new political philosophy.[13]

THE AMERICAN EXPERIENCE

The American revolution took place when the people in the eastern colonies rebelled against British rule and on 4 July 1776 issued a declaration which stated:

> We hold these Truths to be self-evident, that all Men are created equal and are endowed by their Creator with certain inalienable Rights, that among these are Life, Liberty and the Pursuit of Happiness.[14]

Thirteen years later the American constitution was framed, and became the first written national constitution in the world. In contrast to the radical nature of the revolution itself, the constitution was a conservative document which reflected the compromise between democratic and anti-democratic forces in the Congress. Most of those who participated in the constitutional convention were the property-owning, upper-middle-class citizens. The small farmers and the labouring classes were virtually unrepresented since less than 5% of the men had the right to vote. Almost immediately the constitution was revised, and the first ten amendments became known as the Bill of Rights. They expanded some of the declaration's earlier statements concerning the rights to freedom of speech and of the press, "the right of the people to be secure in their persons, houses, papers and effects, against unreasonable searches and seizures",[15] and the right to the free exercise of religion.

The American independence struggle has a special position in history since it was the first successful liberation movement to defeat a European colonial power. In this sense it has been a model for many subsequent struggles of countries under colonial rule. A striking example of this is seen in the proclamation of Vietnamese independence on 2 September 1945. The introductory words are: "All men are created equal. They are endowed by the Creator with certain inalienable rights; among these are life, liberty and the pursuit of happiness." This direct quotation from the American Declaration of Independence indicates the intellectual familiarity of Ho Chi Minh with the spirit of Thomas Jefferson and the American revolution.[16]

BEGINNINGS IN EUROPE

That revolution was one of the many factors which exacerbated the revolution of France. The high cost of French support for General Washington had boosted taxes and was a cause for discontent, and the revolutionary ideas of the new republicanism in America had helped to give focus to the discontent. On 14 July 1789, the poor people of Paris took to the streets and stormed the Bastille. It was a revolution of the masses who rallied under the call for liberty, fraternity and equality. Under pressure from the people, the Constituent National Assembly met on the night of 4 August 1789, and legislated the feudal system out of existence.

In "The Declaration of the Rights of Man and of Citizens" there is the framework of the people's revolution.[17] The great declaration began with the announcement: "Men are born free, and remain free and equal in their rights", but immediately it followed with a compromise clause which reads: "Social distinctions shall be based solely on the common good." Clearly, the bourgeois drafters of the declaration were not going to let the moment of their triumph slip from them, and the qualifying clauses were a way of using the society's confusion to protect middle-class vested interests; for it was they who would determine what was "the common good".

Barely four years afterwards, in the autumn of 1793, the number of prisoners held for political reasons in Paris alone was about 8,000. "This number does not include those held in different dungeons all over France. Between spring 1793 and autumn 1794 more than 3,000 people were guillotined for political reasons. Robespierre deemed it indispensable to cut down the 'internal enemies', in order to save the republic, the revolution and liberty."[18] The revolution had been betrayed by its own leadership.

The French revolution abruptly ended the feudal privileges, laws and institutions of France. It summed up a Europe-wide trend, and inspired the bourgeoisie and peasantry in other European countries to follow. These people welcomed Napoleon in his initial military conquests, because he helped dismantle the feudal structure of each conquered territory. However, since this was done from above and not by the masses, the reforms were seldom permanent. Much of 19th century European history deals with the continuing struggle between the liberal reformers and the feudal forces of the status quo.

The liberal tradition gave rise to a series of ideas about man and society which established the predominant ideology of modern western society. The discovery of the person as a psychological reality who had some rights and integrity as well as duties was expressed in political forms of democracy, the nation state, the capitalist system and free enterprise. According to Martin Buber, it also helped to bring on a major modern crisis, which he calls the decay of old organic forms of the direct life of man with man. By these he means the small communities such as family, union in work, village and town. "Their increasing decay is the price that had to be paid for man's political liberation in the French Revolution and for the subsequent establishment of a bourgeois society."[19]

Liberalism, therefore, came to the people as an amalgam of ideas. It established certain individual rights which were available for every citizen, yet in practice these were not often applied; it gave rise to a bourgeoisie which, in turn, became the foundation of western commerce and industry, with immense benefits to many but exploitation of many others; it introduced the decay of small communities, but gave the possibility of individual development and the growth of cities. The liberal revolution came at a time when society was regarded as a collection of individuals whose rights needed protection. In trying to meet the rights of the individual, it raised other complex social questions about the nature of a just society.

In the next 150 years liberal thought was refined and developed. This process coincided with the expansion of the colonial rule of European nations and its related debates on how to govern the indigenous people, the rights of minorities, the use of slaves and the extraction of vassal tribute. Internationalism in politics was unknown, but coalitions took place among colonizing powers to deal with fractious colonies or (as in the case of the Ottoman Empire) when excesses offended moral sensitivity. The industrial revolution with the emergence of a labouring class changed the nature of the western world and raised new questions about fair wages, working conditions, the right to strike and allied industrial issues.

Marxism and the rights of the people

The Marxist philosophy was a frontal attack on the liberal view of man. Marx rejected the 18th century statements on the rights of man as being a bourgeois illusion which simply reinforced the position of the elite and did nothing to support the masses in their class struggle. The French Revolution, he claimed, abolished feudal property only to favour bourgeois property.[20]

The priority of economic development within political theory makes Marx deal at length with property rights in the "Manifesto of the Communist Party".

> We Communists have been reproached with the desire of abolishing the right of personally acquiring property as the fruit of man's own labour... but in our existing society, private property is already done away with for nine-tenths of the population; its existence for the few is solely due to its non-existence in the hands of the nine-tenths.[21]

In communism, man is never seen as an isolated competitive being surrounded by his own empire of rights. Marx sees man as *Gattungswesen*, a species-being who shares insights as well as duties with his fellow beings.[22] Humans are characterized by the fact that the individual is a part of the state and society. He takes part in the total social and political construction of the state and contributes to the common good. The Soviet Russian revolution of 1917 put Marxist theory to practice and was the precursor of communist expansion.

Under the Soviet constitution of the USSR guarantees of free speech and freedom of assembly were listed, but the 1936 revision went a step further and offered the people positive means for retaining their rights. On the question of the freedom of expression, for example, the constitution offered to turn over to the working people "all technical and material means for the publication of newspapers, pamphlets and books".[23] The Soviet model speaks little of defending rights, but offers facilities for defence of rights and promises freedom in their use. As with so many human rights statements, in the reality of praxis we find that compliance with the ideals seldom occurs. At the time when the revised constitution was being approved, Stalin had just finished his 18 months' special interrogation of the party leaders and begun the great purge. The Russian constitution, no less than the American and the French, was a captive of its political system.

The Chinese application of Marxism also spoke of freedom and equality, but did not recognize the universality of these rights.

> The workers, peasants, Red Army soldiers and the entire toiling population shall have the right to elect their own deputies to give effect to their power. Only militarists, bureaucrats, landlords, the gentry, village bosses, monks — all exploiting and counter-revolutionary elements — shall be deprived of the right.[24]

Mao tse Tung who led the new China was motivated by a belief in the goodness of the masses and a distrust of intellectuals. The values that mark the Maoist vision of a new man and a new society are to be found in the common people.

The understanding of human rights must be seen in the light of the basic contradictions of society, summed up in the phrase: "Who are our friends — who are our enemies?" The first Constitution infers that the enemies include the rightist and counter-revolutionary forces. Since the recent exposure of the so-called

Gang of Four, China has also recognized the possibility of "left-ist" errors as well. Once these enemies of the people have been exposed, it is the duty of the state to re-educate them. The description "political prisoners" has no meaning in China, since there are no prisons, only places for re-education.

There are many restrictions on individual freedom in modern China. Freedom of movement, of speech and of choice of work is almost unknown. The indiscriminate voicing of a political opinion is not possible. Yet with all these restrictions, the way in which basic human needs of food, clothing and housing have been met remains an impressive achievement. The Chinese position on human rights is to narrow the gap in the inequalities of society.

The Marxist revolutions in Europe and Asia have posed the sharpest challenge to the liberal understanding of human rights. Their position has tended to polarize the debate so that it becomes one of the rights of the society versus the rights of the individual. This is not a helpful distinction, although it is widely used in international political debate. Neither extreme is possible. A society cannot exist without the individuals who comprise it, and no person can have rights in isolation from the rights of the society. To divide the two positions into "either-or" is to destroy the validity of both.

The international declarations

We come next to the area which has been both the most creative and, at the same time, the most frustrating in recent concern for human rights. This is the attempt to explicate human rights by means of international declarations and protocols. The movement emerged simultaneously in Europe and America, and was the western world's response to the horrors of the 1939-1945 war. Peace was seen to be necessary for each nation in order to "defend life, liberty, independence and religious freedom and to preserve human rights and justice in their own lands as well as in other lands".[25] The institutional form through which this formidable commission was to be achieved was the United Nations (UN).

For the first three years in the life of the UN the search for a declaration of human rights absorbed the energies of some of the best international lawyers and politicians in the western world. Reading their reflections, one can capture the missionary zeal with which they operated. "We believed that nothing was more needful in a world which had just emerged from a most devastating war... than to capture and affirm the full integrity of man."[26] It was an intoxicating event for many people when the "Universal Declaration of Human Rights" was eventually presented on 10 December 1948.[27] By the 20th anniversary of its signing it had been officially translated into 80 languages and was written into or quoted in the constitutions of 40 nations.[28]

UNIVERSAL DECLARATION OF HUMAN RIGHTS

The declaration reverses the trend of the earlier liberal declarations. Whereas these asserted freedom *from* certain restrictions and oppressions, the "Universal Declaration" takes the next step and asserts some positive rights. That is, the people have rights to some things by virtue of being human. These include education, a reasonable standard of living and health care. The weakness of this new interpretation of rights is that while they appear similar, the co-relative duty for their observance does not rest with humanity at large, nor with any particular person.[29] To say, for example, that "everyone has the right to social security" [30] is not the same as saying that the government has the obligation or duty to supply this. Indeed, there are those who would argue the contrary.

The declaration is thus not an obligatory assertion for all people but rather a referral point or, as it states itself, "a common standard of achievement". It gives the people a list of basic needs and reasonable expectations. Its chief value to date lies in being an internationally accepted statement to which people who are oppressed or are victims of human rights violations can appeal, or which can be used as the lever to enforce reforms in society. It is a programme for society, a conception of what life could be like if humans were treated with dignity and respect. It is "the corollary of the equally modern notion of social justice."[31]

The basis on which the United Nations operates is the concept of the nation-state. It has become axiomatic in international conferences and declarations to exalt the nation as the supreme body for all functional operations. This creates considerable conflict for the international community when it comes to treat questions of human rights, because it is inherent in such rights that they are universal, and therefore beyond the boundaries of the nation-state. No matter how morally offensive a nation's activities may be, the international community cannot intervene, because of the conditional clauses in the UN Charter.

This weakness in the "Universal Declaration" has been evident since it was drawn up, and a mechanism for implementing human rights became a central concern of the General Assembly. The drafts for an international bill of rights were debated for 12 years by the UN before they were finally adopted in 1966. This bill consists of two covenants and an optional protocol.[32] Implementation is mainly through a system by which nations are required to send reports for consideration by the Commission on Human Rights. Each country makes its own reporting, so sessions tend to become a tiresome recital of achievements. Anticipating this, some nations have ratified the optional protocol which gives power to the commission to receive direct communication from individuals and groups who claim to be the victims of human rights violations. The process by which this operates is also cumbersome and requires the person to exhaust all possible domestic remedies first — a task which is somewhat daunting to people who are already victims of oppression.

THE POLITICAL OUTWEIGHS THE MORAL

The United Nations, in fact, has very few resources for action beyond the sphere of moral persuasion. A nation's leader may blatantly and consistently engage in inhumane acts, but the international community is impotent, chiefly because of the political implications of any action. One of the levels at which this situation is most acute is the right of a people to self-determination. This was the point of greatest conflict in the debate over the UN "Covenant on Civil and Political Rights". Who are the people who have the right to self-determination? In Bangladesh the rights of the people were systematically violated by the Pakistan military in 1971. This was internationally known and condemned, but the UN was unable to intervene. Bangladesh won its freedom from this particular oppression through the barrels of the guns of the Indian army. On the other hand, a move for independence on the part of Biafra, 1968-1970, was crushed by the military and no country was prepared to prevent this.

In both cases a large and self-contained section of a nation desired self-determination, but in neither case did the international community act with strength, and in neither case did the fact that the UN had issued a widely-accepted clause supporting the rights of the people to self-determination carry any pragmatic meaning.[33] The result differed in the two cases solely because in one unilateral military action was taken by a friendly neighbour, probably out of national self-interest but it forced a military solution. Whether a people have a right or not seems to emerge from political and military power rather than the moral force of the UN resolutions.

The role of the church

Where has the church been during the people's struggle to attain their rights? There are four possible perspectives for handling this question:

1. From the viewpoint of the people we could interpret the way in which socio-political change "had sparked an experience among the masses which sought for religious expression... through the only symbolic system available, that of Christianity".[34] In early European movements, this was a relevant factor in the people's struggle and today, in countries with a strong Christian tradition, the masses still seek the symbols of revolution within Christian life and terminology, often to the distress of the official churches. Examples of this are the Negro civil rights movement in the United States and the Christian symbols of liberation in Latin America.

2. Again, from the people's perspective, we could analyse their attitudes towards religious institutions. In the Marxist revolution in Soviet Russia, for example, these played a significant role. Officially, Marxism saw Christianity as a bourgeois illusion, an opiate for the people, and many who fought in the revolution regarded the church, especially the Orthodox Church, as a symbol of the decadence of the former feudal state. But this view is full of ambiguities, because large sections of the people retained a deep commitment to institutional forms of the church.

3. A third possibility is to see the question through the statements and resolutions of church assemblies. Almost every major denomination and ecumenical agency has debated questions related to human rights in the last 20 years, and this has provided a verbal mountain of resolutions. However, we can discern within them a recurrent thread which reflects a trend in the theological thought of the church.

4. A final possibility is to see the question interpreted through the words and actions of those individuals and groups who, from a Christian motivation, are working directly with poor and oppressed people in the struggle to attain full human dignity. Within the church, this is a counter-culture group variously identified by such labels as "social activists" or "frontier ministries".

Neither of these stereotypes does justice either to the groups or to the rest of the church which should itself be both active about social concerns and live on the frontier of faith and non-faith. We will, instead, use the word "sodality", an ancient term meaning an association, especially of a religious character. This word has the advantage of neutrality and is not prejudicially loaded.

First WCC statement

In this section we consider the role of the church as it appears in the third option, and interpret the broad stream of Christian witness to human rights reflected in the life of the World Council of Churches (WCC) in the past 30 years. The fourth option will be considered in the next chapter.

The founding of the WCC in 1948 coincided with the secular world's struggle to formulate the "Universal Declaration of Human Rights", and the Council became directly involved through the work of its agency, the Churches Commission on International Affairs (CCIA). The mandate for this commission had been determined at a conference in 1946 and read in part: "Encouragement of, respect for, and observance of human rights and fundamental freedoms, special attention being given to the problem of religious liberty."[35] Previous missionary conferences in 1937 and 1938 had focused the churches' attention on religious liberty, which was regarded as one of the "essential conditions necessary to the church's fulfilment of its primary duty",[36] and so, when the WCC was inaugurated in Amsterdam, one of its major statements was the "Declaration on Religious Liberty."[37]

This still remains one of the best interpretations of the meaning of religious freedom. It avoids the worst expressions of triumphalism, although it comes close to this in the introduction. There are four clauses: individual rights to determine faith and creed; rights for worship and their implications; religious association; and rights to determine policies and practices. The weakest point is where it considers the right to change one's religion. This receives only a brief and passing mention in clause one, but in many countries, particularly where Islam and Christianity coexist, the adoption of a new religion has been the most formidable question of religious freedom.

The controversy in the next years centred around the phrase "freedom of religion". It was a phrase which western Christians, including such a spokesman as president Roosevelt, had used too loosely, and often interchangeably, with "freedom of worship". The Russian foreign minister, Mr Molotov, was willing to accept "freedom of religious worship" but considered "freedom of religion" would be unacceptable to the USSR.[38] A compromise wording appeared in the UN final declaration, and Article 18 reads:

> Everyone has the right to freedom of thought, conscience and religion; this right includes freedom to change his religion or belief, and freedom, either alone or in community with others and in public or private, to manifest his religion or belief in teaching, practice, worship and observance.[39]

THE PEOPLE, NOT THE CHURCH

For the next 20 years, international Christian attention remained focused on religious freedoms as they were being defined in the covenants. Throughout this whole period, until the New Delhi assembly in 1961, there is little evidence that the wider questions of human rights were given much serious attention by the churches. It is hard to avoid the conclusion that this epoch was one of institutional self-protectionism. Church social action at the international level concentrated on the one-way flow of refugees from communist countries to the West and a concept of inter-church aid motivated by the expectation that the transfer of charitable gifts from the rich to the poor would balance the world's resources and serve the cause of justice. A more comprehensive theology of international justice and human dignity was required before the churches could look at human rights in a holistic way.

At New Delhi, an assembly of the World Council of Churches met in a developing nation for the first time. The delegates were faced with the reality of the rich-poor dichotomy each time they left their hotel. Another long statement on religious liberty was approved, but it broke no new ground.[40] However, it linked human rights with questions of justice, and the report spoke of improved economic conditions, racial discrimination and injustice. The pre-eminence of human dignity was beginning to assert itself. Racism questions also appeared high on the assembly agenda and were a reminder of a specific aspect of the human rights violations in many nations.

The Uppsala assembly in 1968 coincided with the 20th anniversary of the signing of the "Universal Declaration of Human Rights" and, by this time, the two protective covenants had also been finalized. The assembly used the occasion to look at its human rights action retrospectively, and give a contemporary interpretation. Following the two major speeches, those who took the floor to comment ignored the statements which had been made and used the time to vigorously press for specific human rights causes.[41] These included such issues as: relations between Armenians and Jews; the supply of arms to Nigeria; relief to Biafra; discrimination against women; and violence in the Congo. It was a signal that the churches were moving into a new stage in their understanding of human rights. Their concerns had become less church-centred and more person-centred, with the result that specific local violations of rights had precedence in delegates' thoughts.

By 1968 the churches' emphasis on social justice had led to a new and controversial programme to combat racism, plus a strong mandate to participate in development programmes. Both were built into the operational structure of the WCC and helped the evolution of new theological thought about justice. The focus of God's concern was to be the people and not the church. The presence of the poor and the oppressed was a scandal to human conscience and at Uppsala churches began to realize that this must be attacked not at the level of its results, but at the root causes. A statement on the "Protection of Individuals and Groups in the Political World" was approved, and while it does not deal in depth with political dynamics, it does begin to look at human rights in a wider perspective.[42]

NAIROBI: MAJOR DEBATES

Uppsala linked human rights observance with both peace and justice, and thus placed it at the centre of the WCC's social concern. Although no clear mandate was given, the CCIA immediately engaged upon a human rights study, culminating its efforts with a consultation at St Polten, Austria, in 1974.[43] Material produced at St Polten was seminal to the development of human rights as a primary concern for the WCC. At the Nairobi assembly in December 1975 the issues emerged with vigour, although this was heightened by the use of floor amendments during several different human rights debates.

A general statement presented to the assembly on the Helsinki agreement was brought to life when a Swiss delegate, speaking to a resolution about restrictions to religious liberty, proposed an amendment which read "particularly in the USSR."[44] A lively but brief debate, closed prematurely by the chairman, led to a separate hearing to resolve the wording. At this meeting the Russians argued on three main points: western interference would not help their situation; Helsinki was new and needed time for results; singling out the USSR was unfair and unwarranted.[45] The final resolution was predictably neutral, but the debate had opened up more far-reaching issues. The silence of western churches towards human rights questions in the Soviet Republics had been broken for the first time, and the possibility of an open debate on the human rights violations in communist nations had begun to emerge.

A second major debate came with the presentation of the report "Human Rights in Latin America."[46] This comprehensive paper reflected the wide range of Latin American expertise on the WCC's staff as well as the international horror at the gross violations of human rights in these nations. The debate was characteristic of most current church considerations on human rights. On one side were the spokesmen for a much harder line. These were the people who spoke with a prophet's fervour and expressed anger at the dehumanizing events taking place. The other side was represented largely by people from the countries themselves who urged caution and moderation. "This will cause problems for churches and individuals," said the delegate from Brazil.[47] Finally, the assembly accepted a synoptic statement mentioning specifically Chile and Argentina, and also established a fund to assist with human rights concerns in Latin America.

Two other assembly issues can be mentioned briefly. In one, a delegate sought to have included a reference to several Asian nations in a general resolution about human rights.[48] Opposition came because the amendment was selective in nature and used some words which were not acceptable. A sub-committee met to make it more comprehensive, and the reformulated text was accepted by the assembly. In the second event, a resolution concerning East Timor was sharpened when an Australian delegate proposed an amendment to the statement, referring to Indonesian troops being removed.[49] This alarmed the Indonesian delegation, and although the resolution was passed it caused lingering suspicion and recrimination between the neighbouring churches in Indonesia and Australia.

POTENTIALLY EXPLOSIVE DEBATE

Each of these incidents is a manifestation of the contemporary mood to give contextual significance to the human rights debate. Earlier assemblies discussed religious rights and, sometimes, human rights, but often in vacuum. With the coming of the Programme to Combat Racism, countries began to be named by the churches, and this brought the predictable reactionary statements from politicians and church leaders. The WCC was accused of "selective indignation", and the standard response of any country to accusations of racism was to divert attention to another country rather than accept a national responsibility.

The debate on human rights in the forums of international Christian life is potentially even more explosive than racism questions. Racism is not only a political and economic issue but can also be interpreted in social terms. Thus, most Christians can accept that there is some moral necessity for Christians to speak on a racism question. When we come to human rights, however, we are often dealing with an issue presented as almost wholly political. To raise the question of political prisoners, for example, is to speak of persons designated by their government as subversive. If a group passes a resolution asking for the release of such prisoners, governments will consider this an intrusion into their internal affairs, and it will be construed as an unfriendly political action.

Nairobi, therefore, opened up a threatening issue which, if pursued, will cause greater strains on the WCC fellowship than any of its previous programmes. Unless discussion is stifled, the Council's next assembly will be under intense pressure to debate specific national situations involving political repression, denials of freedom and cases of dehumanizing behaviour. An open debate on these themes, if it became localized, has the potential to neutralize the effectiveness of international church relationships.

NOTES

[1] Ian McGregor: *Human Rights*. London: Batsford, 1975, p. 18.

[2] Egon Schwelb: "Human Rights." In *Encyclopaedia Britannica*, 15th ed., 1975, Macropaedia 8, p. 1183.

[3] Great Britain: "The Magna Carta," Clause 39.

[4] D. C. Somervell: *A Concise History of Great Britain*. London: Bell, 1928, p. 47.

5 Mencius: "The Counsels of Kao-Yao" (Book of Yu, III). In *The Wisdom of China and India*, ed. Lin Yutang. New York: The Modern Library, 1968, p. 720.

6 Mencius: Book of History. Book VII, Part II, Chapter XIV, In Yutang, *ibid.*, p. 784.

7 Mencius: Book of History. Book VI, Part II, Chapter II. In Yutang, *ibid.*, p. 782.

8 C. P. Fitzgerald: *A Concise History of East Asia*. London: Penguin, 1974, p. 67.

9 Nigel Cameron: *From Bondage to Liberation: East Asia 1860-1952*. Hong Kong: Oxford University Press, 1975, p. 67.

10 *Ibid.*, p. 61.

11 Mark Sunder Rao: "Religious Movements and Social Transformation in India." In *Religion and Development in Asian Societies*. Colombo, Sri Lanka: Marga Publications, 1974, p. 131.

12 John Locke (1632-1704): *Two Treatises of Government*, ed. P. P. Lasset, Cambridge, 1960; *A Letter Concerning Toleration*, London, 1689 — Adam Smith (1723-1790): *The Wealth of Nations*, London, Pelican, 1974 — John Stuart Mill (1806-1873): *Essay on Liberty*, London, Pelican, 1972 — F.-M. Arouet de Voltaire (1694-1778): *Siècle de Louis XIV*, Paris, 1751 — Denis Diderot (1713-1784): *Dialogues*, trans. F. Birrell, New York, 1927 — Jean-Jacques Rousseau (1712-1778): *Political Writings*, ed. C. A. Vaughan, Cambridge, 1915 — Wolfgang von Goethe (1749-1832): *Faust*, trans. W. Kauffman, New York, 1961 — Immanuel Kant (1724-1804): *The Moral Law*, trans. H. J. Paton, London, 1948 — Benjamin Franklin (1706-1790): *Autobiography*, New Haven, 1964 — Thomas Paine (1737-1809): *The Rights of Man*, ed. Henry Collins, London, Pelican Classics, 1976.

13 Henry Collins' introduction to Thomas Paine: *The Rights of Man*, *op. cit.*, p. 15.

14 US General Congress: "A Declaration by the Representatives of the United States of America", 4 July 1776, para. 2.

15 US Constitution: Amendment (IV), proposed US Congress, 25 September 1789.

16 Jean Lacouture: *Ho Chi Minh*, trans. Peter Wiles. London: Penguin, 1969, p. 224.

17 National Assembly of France: "Declaration of the Rights of Man and of Citizens", 27 August 1789. *Encyclopaedia Britannica*, *op. cit.*, Macropaedia 7, pp. 650-651.

18 Julio Barreiro: "In Defence of Human Rights." *The Ecumenical Review*, WCC, Vol. XXVII, No. 2, 1975, p. 106. He comments: "To be quite candid, in modern history human rights have never been proclaimed for the purpose of being respected or implemented."

19 Martin Buber: *Between Man and Man*. London: Fontana, 1974, p. 192.

20 Karl Marx: "The Eighteenth Brumaire of Louis Bonaparte." In *Marx and Engels, Basic Writings*, ed. Lewis S. Feuer. London: Collins, 1974, p. 360 f. Also Frederick Engels: "On Historical Materialism." *Ibid.*, p. 98 f.

[21] "Manifesto of the Communist Party", English version of 1888. *Ibid.*, p. 63-64.

[22] Maurice Cranston: *What Are Human Rights?* London: Bodley Head, 1973, p. 75.

[23] Soviet Government of USSR: "Declaration of the Rights of the Working and Exploited People", 19 July 1918. Revised in 1936 under Josef Stalin; further revisions in 1963 and 1977.

[24] "Constitution of the (Chinese) Soviet Republic", 7 November 1931, para. 2. In Donald E. MacInnis: *Religious Policy and Practice in Communist China.* New York: Macmillan, 1972, p. 19.

[25] Joint declaration of United Nations, 1 January 1942, signed by 26 nations. In O. Frederick Nolde: *Free and Equal.* Geneva: WCC, 1968, p. 19.

[26] Charles Malik, introduction to Nolde, *ibid.*, p. 7.

[27] United Nations, General Assembly, 10 December 1948: "Universal Declaration of Human Rights." Voting: 48 for, 0 against, 8 abstained, 2 absent. In *The United Nations and Human Rights.* New York: UN, 1973, p. 12.

[28] O. Frederick Nolde: "Human Rights in Retrospect: a Contemporary Appraisal." *The Ecumenical Review*, Geneva, Vol. XX, No. 4, October 1968, pp. 395-403.

[29] Stanley I. Benn: "Human Rights." In *The Encyclopaedia of Philosophy.* New York: Macmillan, 1967, Vol. VII, p. 197.

[30] United Nations: "Universal Declaration of Human Rights." Article 25.

[31] Stanley I. Benn. *Op. cit.*, Vol. VII, p. 198.

[32] United Nations, General Assembly, 16 December 1966: "Covenant on Economic, Social and Cultural Rights." Voting: 105 for, 0 against. "Covenant on Civil and Political Rights." Voting: 106 for, 0 against. "Optional Protocol to the Covenant on Civil and Political Rights." Voting: 66 for, 2 against, 38 abstained. In *The United Nations and Human Rights*, *op. cit.*, p. 81.

[33] Maurice Cranston, *op. cit.*, p. 60.

[34] François Houtart and André Rousseau: *The Church and Revolution.* New York: Orbis, 1971, p. 53.

[35] Conference of Church Leaders on International Affairs, Cambridge, England, 4-7 August 1946. In *The Ten Formative Years 1938-1948.* Geneva: WCC, 1948, p. 58.

[36] Oxford Conference on Church, Community and State, July 1937. In *The Churches in International Affairs.* Geneva: WCC/CCIA, 1974. The conference in 1938 was the Tambaram-Madras, India, International Missionary Conference.

[37] "Declaration on Religious Liberty", adopted by the WCC and the International Missionary Council, in the Netherlands, 1948. In O. Frederick Nolde: *Free and Equal, op. cit.*, pp. 79-81.

[38] *Ibid.*, p. 34.

[39] United Nations, General Assembly. "Universal Declaration of Human Rights." Article 18.

40 "Human Rights and Religious Liberty." In *The New Delhi Report.* Geneva: WCC, 1961, pp. 276-279.

41 O. Frederick Nolde: "Human Rights in Retrospect: a Contemporary Appraisal", and Robert R. K. A. Gardiner: "Christianity and Human Rights." *The Ecumenical Review*, Geneva, Vol. XX, No. 4, October 1968, pp. 395-403 and pp. 404-409.

42 *The Uppsala Report.* Geneva: WCC, 1968, pp. 63-67.

43 Consultation on Human Rights, St Polten, Austria, 21-26 October 1974. *Human Rights and Christian Responsibility.* Geneva: WCC, 1974.

44 David M. Paton, ed.: *Breaking Barriers: Nairobi 1975.* London: SPCK, and Grand Rapids: Eerdmans, 1976, pp. 169-172.

45 Albert H. van den Heuvel: "The Churches and Human Rights." *Mid Stream*, Council on Christian Unity of the Christian Church (Disciples of Christ), Indianapolis, USA, Vol. XVI, No. 2, April 1977, p. 222.

46 David M. Paton, *op. cit.*, pp. 177-179.

47 *Ibid.*, p. 178.

48 *Ibid.*, pp. 98 and 100.

49 *Ibid.*, pp. 175-177.

III. The church and human rights in Asia

The historical forces which have brought us to this moment in history have driven us to ask many new questions about the meaning of human rights. Within the Asian region we experience this dynamic in some unexpected ways as cultural, religious, economic and political forces juggle with the lives of the people.

To those of us who work within Asia the diversity means it is difficult to make any statement without an immediate qualification. We speak of the deprivation of the poorest people on earth, and must then concede that some of the wealthiest pockets of humanity also live within the Asian region. We speak of eastern "mysticism" and "spirituality", only to be reminded of the pragmatic and hard-headed Asian business executives who can out-manœuvre and undercut the toughest western traders. We speak of "Asian" attitudes towards freedom, towards the family, towards political leaders, towards money, and must then qualify our comments in such a way as to make them meaningless. In such a pluralistic society the answers to many of our questions about human rights are complex and qualified.

Christianity has lived uneasily with this pluralism for many centuries. Currently, there are almost 100 million Christians in the whole Asian area, and they can therefore lay claim to being one of the main religions of the region. However, apart from areas of strong Christian influence in the Philippines or in parts of Indonesia and India, the actual Christian presence is very small. In several countries Christians constitute less than 1% of the population.[1]

Asian Christians have been deeply affected by being a minority religion. During colonialism they were often placed in a position of privilege out of all proportion to their size. Despite their small numbers, they were a dominant minority.

In the post-independence era, Christians have played a key role in several countries, largely because of their better education, facility with foreign languages, contacts with overseas organizations, and their ownership of hospitals, schools and similar institutions. Christians used to say that although they were few their influence was considerable, and so they used the phrase "creative minority".

More recently, the Christians have lost many positions of authority, and their sources of power are being confiscated by the state. A series of other events have begun to suggest to the church that it is also not very creative. A more appropriate description for these Christians at the present time might be a "nervous minority".

Of all the forces which threaten the minority churches in Asia, few create such ambivalent response as human rights. While recognizing that there are violations of human dignity which demand protest and response, the church is nevertheless caught in the dilemma that such action can threaten its survival. There is no doubt that in every Asian nation there are examples of quite extreme human rights violations and many Christians feel greatly anguished about such events, but the argument of expediency makes much of the church leadership silent and impotent.

Indonesia is an example of one such country. Whenever human rights is mentioned in the West, Indonesia is cited as the country in which there are more political prisoners than any other Asian nation. There is evidence that Christian leaders there are distressed at the prisoners' plight and have taken some steps to assist them. But apart from a handful of Christians, the church has been silent and even defensive when the issue has been raised in international debate. Its leaders will explain that public action would risk the very survival of the church, because extremist Muslim groups would use it to build up persecution or other anti-Christian feeling.

In other Asian nations, the minority church has to co-exist with a communist rule. This poses its own problems. In Vietnam in 1975 the Christians, largely Roman Catholic, numbered 10% of the population, and in Laos 1.4%. In the People's Republic of China the number is unknown. In Kampuchea (the former Cambodia) numbers are negligible; perhaps 10,000 persons, at most, out of a population of eight million.

In these situations, the role of the church in human rights is defined by the exigencies of the state. It is clear that communism places great restrictions on personal freedoms, and on many communal freedoms. Freedom of speech, of travel, and the right to protest are all heavily curtailed. Asian visitors to each of the communist countries have spoken with church leaders, and sometimes there have been privately expressed opinions about these human rights violations. Yet there is a sense of powerlessness

26

which prevents the church from taking any overt social action. Visitors who are sensitive to the issues are prevented from speaking openly afterwards, because this could only cause greater suffering to the Christian community who have to continue to try and be faithful under communist rule.

Asia is a continent of amazing social ferment, and each nation is still experimenting with the possibilities of government. In addition to the communist states there are varieties of socialism, guided democracies, emergency rule, martial law, military dictatorships, capitalist-socialism, and many other shades of rule. For almost every country, the liberation from colonialism is the definitive historical event of recent years, and it is within this heady experience of freedom that they are still struggling to find the way to survive.

It is the role of the small, sometimes fearful, and often ineffective Christian community to witness to human values in societies where these are being disregarded or abused.

In the next three sections we will look at the way the church has responded in specific national situations.

Case Study One: the Myong Dong 18

In the Chinese cultural tradition, which has dominated northern and eastern Asia, the clearest expression of the people's aspirations has been through popular peasant movements. The folk history of these events has interpreted them with a strong moralizing overtone. "Peasant rebellion and other popular revolts in traditional Asia often formulated religious and social doctrines to legitimize their demands." [2] Yet this was a surface expression which hid the real reasons for the revolt: the deep social discontent and the people's anxiety to find their own freedom and dignity. The T'aip'ing revolution, as we have indicated, cannot be seen as just a religious movement; it was also an assertion by the people of their humanity.

The 1862-1863 Tonghak peasant rebellion in Korea was a movement for social transformation based on religious principles. [3] It was the inspiration and forerunner of many subsequent movements of which the 1 March 1919 Independence Movement was the most important.

In 1919 Korea was a subject state of Japan and the victim of widespread oppression. On 1 March of that year, a group of religious leaders issued a statement calling for national independence. Thirty-three prominent Koreans signed this statement, which drew an immediate response from the people. A peaceful demonstration in Seoul was attended by 50,000 Koreans, and a movement for independence swept through the country. After two months, the Japanese rulers, feeling endangered, ordered a cruel suppression. According to Japanese estimates, 533 Koreans were killed, 1,409 injured and 19,054 imprisoned,[4] but the total of Koreans killed and wounded probably reached 23,000 with about 47,000 arrested.[5] The events left an indelible impression on the minds of the Korean people, and once independence was achieved, March 1 was declared an annual public holiday.

ACCUSATION OF CORRUPTION

The year 1976 marked the 57th anniversary of the 1 March uprising. As in previous years, services of worship and thanksgiving took place all over the country. In Myong Dong cathedral, Seoul, a service sponsored by the National League of Catholic Priests for the Realization of Justice was held. It lasted three-and-a-half hours and during that time sermons were preached by the Rev. Moon Dong Hwan, former professor of missiology at Hankuk Seminary, and Father Kim Sung Hun, a 37 year-old Catholic priest. The congregation also heard a letter of appeal from the mother of imprisoned poet Kim Chi Ha. As the service concluded Miss Lee Oo Jung, the president of Korea's Church Women United and a former professor of New Testament at Seoul Women's College, read a statement entitled "Declaration for Democratic National Salvation".[6]

The reading of statements and declarations on special occasions is a traditional activity in Korean churches. Some of the earlier statements have come to be regarded with veneration as modern creeds. The "Theological Declaration of Korean Christians" in 1973,[7] for example, is widely quoted as one of the more important theological affirmations to emerge from Asia in recent years. To read a declaration in the service at Myong Dong was not exceptional and would normally provoke no comment.

The "Declaration for Democratic National Salvation" was almost 2,000 words in length, and contained an historical survey of the people's struggle for liberation; an affirmation of the value of the democratic system; an economic assessment which spoke of corruption originating in the very heart of the power structure; and finally, a section on the reunification of Korea.

The accusation of corruption was one of the main factors causing a strong government reaction to the document. The Korean government has recognized that it rules by strong measures, but justifies this on the grounds of national security and the need for economic development. It is in the latter field that it feels it has achieved the greatest success, with a rise in the per capita GNP and a high growth rate in the industrial sector. To be accused by the declaration of corruption at the point where it feels its greatest contribution has been made is to question the integrity and legitimacy of all other government action.

Added weight was given to the document by the seniority of the signatories. The leader of the opposition, Kim Dae Jung, aged 51, and a former president of Korea, Yun Po Sun, aged 79, were the two best-known figures. University and seminary professors, a former foreign minister, a Quaker leader and a clergyman made up the list. Following interrogation, ten of the signatories were arrested, and they were joined by an additional eight persons who were said to have assisted in the drafting, printing or distribution of the declaration. On 26 March 1976, the Seoul district prosecutor's office indicted 18 persons and charged that the issuing of the declaration was designed to "incite the audience to set off a demonstration which would ignite a general insurrection that spreading would throw the society into confusion, so that they could seize the opportunity to overthrow the present administration and capture the government".[8]

The government of Park Chung Hee warned that "it would not allow Christian churches to be used for political opposition".[9]

THEOLOGICAL SOPHISTICATION

The defendants were a multifarious group representing several different professions — lawyer, priest, writer, teacher — and they had reached their position on the declaration by various paths. The common factor uniting them was that they were all Christians. They did not come from the same denominational stream, but were divided between Presbyterian and Roman Catholic, with one Methodist and one Quaker in the group. It is the Christian homogeneity of the defendants which gives this trial a special place in the history of the church in Asia. As the 18 defendants presented their defence there were times when the courtroom was like a Christian testimony meeting. Without exception, the 18 referred to their Christian faith as the motivation for the stand they had taken.

The defendants spoke twice before crowded courtrooms. The first time was between 26 June and 19 July 1976, when the prosecution interrogated them and each had the right to speak. Just prior to the trial summary there was a second invitation for them to speak, but by this time the defence lawyers had resigned or withdrawn in protest and the defendants were so incensed with the prejudicial order of proceedings that most declined.

In the earlier speeches there were several long statements related to economic and political questions. Complementing these was the defendants' testimony which related to a theological understanding of their position. A summary of the statements is as follows: [10]

— *Goals:* As Christians we do not aspire to power. Our concern is for moral values, and for the life of the people.
— *Social change:* The elimination of social evil requires a change in the social structures, without which individuals cannot be liberated.
— *Church and state:* The church is not to be used by the government, nor should the church try to be the government. Each has its own sphere, but the church must have freedom to act in service to the neighbour, to witness to the truth, to stand for the poor, the weak and the helpless. We remember the Confessing Church in Germany, and think something like that is needed in Korea. A government which rules without moral values becomes a government of gangsters.
— *Human rights:* Jesus always speaks to the issues of basic human rights in a divine dimension; that is the value of each human life. We cannot complain of the denial of human rights in North Korea and sell our society for dollars at the same time.
— *Jesus:* We are required to follow Jesus. If we are imprisoned, we do not mind, because Jesus suffered the same way through righteous activities.
— *People:* What is a nation's strength? In the end it is the people, not the laws or the structures.

This summary indicates the degree of theological sophistication on the part of the defendants. They stand in the best tradition of Christian apologetics with a carefully thought-through position clearly and unashamedly proclaimed.

The government claims that the 18 represent a very small minority both within the society and in the church itself. In the absence of a free society, where such assertions can be tested, there is no way to judge the veracity of such a claim. We know, however, that those who speak publicly are a minority. This leads us to ask: What are the factors which enable a group such as these 18 to act and speak in a way which will inexorably lead to their arrest and imprisonment?

The first clear answer is that the example of the historical Jesus is a most powerful motivating force behind Christian witness. In the Christian faith the Lord who is worshipped identified with the suffering people, went to prison, and died as a common criminal. He has a special compelling power for oppressed believers. The witness of Jesus in his life is the proto-type for the witness of his disciples today. We cannot under-estimate the significance of this. Many of the Myong Dong defend-ants make some acknowledgment of how much this gave them the strength to speak and act as they did. In conversation with the group it also becomes evident that the study of the gospels while in prison has given the 18 the criteria by which they should judge their own witness. The life of Jesus offers a solidarity with oppressed persons which they alone can fully appreciate.

One Korean discovery in recent years is that the concept of human rights speaks a strong and universal language. It may be argued that human rights (certainly in the form in which it developed from the liberal revolution) has subtle western con-notations, but there can also be no doubt that in Korea human rights has a forceful indigenous meaning which brings vigour and incisiveness to the debate on justice. The Korean struggle for independence was the struggle of the people to achieve their place in history and assert their human rights, and the Myong Dong 18 see themselves as fully in that tradition. The Korean National Council of Churches' statement of 26 March 1976, issued in response to the arrests, says:

> The events of 1 March 1976 were not aimed at rebellion but were a continuation of the basic spirit of 1919. The concern was for

human rights and freedom for the whole nation, and therefore the government interpretation is one-sided and exaggerated.[11]

A third factor is the emergence in Korean church life of a strong inner community dedicated to the Christian ideals of justice and social service. The lengthening experience of being a nation under emergency rule has created this diffuse but catalytic fellowship within the life of the whole church. Holding a common theological understanding approximately equivalent to the position of the 18 defendants, this community has provided assurance and support for those on trial. When the arrests were made following the 1 March church service, groups of clergy, students and intellectuals throughout the country prepared statements of support for the 18. The Roman Catholic Bishops of Korea issued a message expressing shock at the arrests [12] and the Korean National Council of Churches made a series of statements.[13] Equally important to the Korean community was the knowledge that throughout the world supportive Christian organizations sent letters, cables and messages of support.

Finally, we note the importance of symbol for the sustaining of the sodality. Quaker leader Hahm Suk Hon signified his objection to the nature of the trial by appearing in court dressed in traditional Korean funeral clothing. As a sign that his allegiance went beyond court proceedings to what he calls his "conscience before God", he remained standing throughout the defence questioning.[14] Another prisoner went on a hunger strike, and the prisoners' wives invented numerous symbolic actions such as wearing a black cross on their lips or sewing a purple cross on their dress.[15] The power of symbol to create community and sustain faith is an important element in the case of the Myong Dong 18.

CHRISTIANITY: A MAJOR ROLE

The faith which is being proclaimed by the 18 defendants of the Myong Dong trial can be described as a theology of the rights of people. In Korean history, Christianity has played a major role in the struggle for liberation and the defence of human rights.

From its 19th century beginning in Korea, the Christian community was rooted in the poorer sections of the population. This thrust the church into the heart of the developing society's social and economic contradictions. Not only through the 1919 events and the Myong Dong 18, but in a wide range of social witness, identification with the peasants, the urban squatters and factory labourers, the church has probed the meaning of Christian witness in a place of oppression. The Christian *koinonia* has been placed in a unique position, since its Christian witness for the rights of the people has made it the nucleus of national concern for the social transformation of the nation.

In the process of fulfilling this mission, the *koinonia* has discovered a wide base of support among the poor and oppressed, and has also established significant international links with similar-minded Christian groups in Asia and the West. Conversely, reactionary groups in the church have protested this stand and sought to neutralize the witness of the Myong Dong 18 by public affirmations in support of repressive measures. The contradictions exist not only in society but also in the church.

Case Study Two: a Radicalized Priest

Father Edicio de la Torre, a Philippine national and priest of the Divine Word Missionaries (SVD), was arrested by the Philippine military on 13 December 1974. A presidential undertaking the same year that any churchmen detained by the authorities would be handed over to their religious superiors for discipline was ignored in this case, because defence secretary Juan Ponce Enrile said that Father de la Torre and another priest, Father Manny Lahoz, were required for questioning. According to secretary Enrile, the crime of the two priests was that they "consorted with people whose primary intention is to overthrow the government or to undermine the stability of society".[16] Legal experts in the Philippines agree that consorting with subversives does not constitute a crime in Philippine law, and in the absence of any formal charge and given the fact that after four years there is still no suggestion of a trial, the general comment of secretary Enrile is the only known "official" statement on their arrest.

The life story of Father de la Torre reveals a gradual escalation of politicized radicalization. Active in student politics during his training, he participated in the founding and programme of the Federation of Free Farmers in the early 1970's. The Federation operated like a farmers' credit union and protected the interests of small landholders or landless workers. With substantial backing from the Roman Catholic Church and support from some international funding agencies, it became a major farmers' programme in the period prior to martial law.

The years 1970-1972 in Philippine history were a time of marked social ferment and revolutionary groups proliferated. A free, and often emotional, press vacillated between responsibility and sensationalism. There was widespread agreement that social change was necessary, and President Marcos was speaking of this when he said that "revolution is inevitable".[17] In his book interpreting his decision to announce martial law, or "crisis government" as it was euphemistically termed, he said:

> The process we need is... revolution by democratic means, the only method of cleansing society and rescuing it from its ills which at the same time preserves, indeed enriches the values that had given life to the social contract.[18]

Throughout this time, the primary objective of Christian sodalities with a social conscience was the social change necessary to redress the glaring economic imbalances existing in Philippine society. Development programmes multiplied as church organizations sought to attack the unjust structures which worked against the rights of the poor. In church circles the methodology of change became the central question, and here the Philippines reflected the issue which was fundamental to Christian social concern in all the developing nations. It came down to the pragmatic question of whether to work for the reform of society from within the existing system or to opt for a radical change in the structures. In the Catholic church this question led to a probing of the Papal Encyclicals, the Christian roots of the church, the history of the Philippines and the experiences of other nations to try and find models for action.

THE FLAME OF LIBERATION THEOLOGY

For many Philippine priests, the search was rewarded with the discovery of the theology of liberation.[19] Emerging from the experience of the church in Latin America, this theological interpretation of the forces which dehumanize developing societies had an added attraction in the Philippines, because the two regions shared a similar Latin and Roman heritage. Liberation theology implies revolutionary change, but it also includes the analysis of the concrete objective forces of oppression. Liberation is from dependence, and this involves not just economic dependence, but also the more subtle forms of cultural and internal dependence. For many priests, liberation theology provided a deeper social analysis than the development theology which preceded it, and its spiritual dimension, for example, liberation from sin and guilt, gave it added respectability for church leaders.

Father de la Torre became a leading Filipino exponent on liberation theology, and for a period was engaged full-time in conducting seminars and retreats on the subject.[20] These led to the formation of a sodality under the name Christians for National Liberation. Founded in February 1972, at a national seminar, the organization became a focal point for Christians seeking the radical renewal of society. Some members of the hierarchy were interested and encouraging, but there was no official endorsement. A few months later, on 21 September 1972, martial law was announced.

Father de la Torre planned to continue lectures and seminars from Christ the King Seminary, where he had become professor of social ethics, but when the military came to arrest him he decided to elude capture and go underground.[21] He travelled secretly to Mindoro to work among the farmers, but soon decided that the main organizational task lay in the cities.

At this time he was approached by leaders of the National Democratic Front (NDF) to become one of their clandestine organizers. The NDF was the major coalition of underground groups working in the Philippines, and their membership included Marxist, Christian and Muslim activists who were ideologically divided but had united to gain the strength to oppose the government forces. Father de la Torre spent several months in this work and in 1974 was offered the chairmanship of the NDF's preparatory committee. After expressing reservations about his competence on the Muslim issue he eventually accepted. While chairman of the NDF he had to work closely with communist leaders, a fact which he never attempted to hide.

In December 1974, after his arrest, Father de la Torre began a well-publicized hunger strike to protest the conditions in prison. Many other prisoners joined him, and after 76 days the fast was lifted when assurances were given to relatives that the abuses would be remedied. Four years have now elapsed, and Father de la Torre is still in prison, writing poetry, painting and, from time to time, managing to have his paintings and letters smuggled to friends in the church outside.

REVOLUTIONARY PRIESTS: A NEW PHENOMENON

Father de la Torre is the most visible of the priests and clergy
in Asia who have opted to identify publicly with those forces
in society which are working for the overthrow of the government
in power and which openly espouse the use of violence in attaining
their ends. The number of clergy who speak publicly of such
violence is quite small. One who has taken an even stronger
stance, but about whom less is known, is Father Louis Jalandoni
of the Philippines, who stated: "I have freely and voluntarily
become a member of the Communist Party... in the light of this,
judge me, my friends, not in the light of what you hear or what
our enemies say, but in the light of our actions and our lives." [22]

Such revolutionary priests are a relatively new phenomenon
in Asia, although they have been known in Africa, southern
Europe and especially in Latin America for some years. Father
Camilo Torres of Colombia is probably the best-known. He
confronts the church with some basic questions about its witness:
"I found that revolution is necessary to feed the hungry and give
drink to the thirsty... I believe that revolutionary combat is a
Christian and priestly combat." [23] Father de la Torre and other
priests in the Philippines stand within this tradition.

It would be presumptuous for outsiders to attempt to discuss
the legitimacy of Father de la Torre's action. An analysis can
only take place within his own church and society. So far the
Catholic church has stood by his right to continue to be a priest.
At the time of his arrest the provincial consultor of the Divine
Word Missionaries issued a statement that the imprisoned
priests' commitment to the poor was the correct pastoral methodology [24] and, at the same time, a circular from the Association
of Major Religious Superiors distributed to every parish in the
Philippines stated that they were "convinced of the value of
their (the priests') witness for justice and truth in love". [25] There
has been equally strong criticism of Father de la Torre's action,
but so far no move to have him defrocked.

Such a man is an embarrassment to the church authorities.
They are forced to face theological, political and psychological
contradictions which are basic to human struggle and which
cannot be solved by compromise or reconciliation. Most would
prefer to avoid confrontation and seek refuge in a strict separation
of church and state. Archbishop Teopiso Alberto, in a pointed
speech in Manila a month after Father de la Torre's arrest, said:

36

> The genuinely loyal citizen is always ready and eager not only to
> observe the laws but to serve, support and maintain the political
> institutions of the country. It means faithful adherence and constant
> allegiance to the sovereignty of the state.[26]

Such a statement would gladden the heart of even the most
despotic ruler, but coming from a clergyman whose first allegiance
is to God and not to the sovereignty of the state it strikes a
discordant note. Christians are not able to support and maintain
a nation's political institutions without some reserve, or else they
will be found upholding the most corrupt and evil regimes.

ALL THE CHOICES ARE WRONG

If we allow the possibility of Christian political action in a
situation of corruption, what are the licit theological actions a
Christian may take? No permanent answer can be given to this
question. All our theological training and experience has not
equipped us for this, one of the most existential questions facing
many Christians today. Put in another way it asks: What is
Christian behaviour in an environment of illegality? In modern
society this is not a simple choice between the law of God and
the law of the state, the *lex Dei* versus the *lex ordinis humani*.
It is more subtle than that. It means being in a situation where
all choices are wrong. In some places it is the confronting of
moral laws which must be broken for conscience sake, and this
causes an inescapable conflict in which no resolution is possible,
because whichever way one acts one is guilty. With the growing
possibility of technocratic controls of society, such situations
must become more numerous.

Iconoclastic priests like Father de la Torre are an acute dis-
comfit for the church. They force the leadership to move into
an unaccustomed place of conflict. It is unaccustomed, because
theologies of reconciliation and "love" have dominated church
politics to the point where the church acts as if it were a neutral
body unrelated to the struggles and suffering of the people. The
conflict model which the radicalized priests thrust on the church
means that neutrality ceases to be an option. The church must
make a decision which cannot be avoided, because even to do
nothing is to make a choice.

Neither the church's teaching nor the example of "prominent"
Christians is helpful in resolving this dilemma. Father de la
Torre and many other Philippine priests who have taken the

radical option have a basic commitment to the poor and the oppressed, and all subsequent choices are to be seen in the light of their primary affirmation. In every conflict situation the question then becomes: What are those choices which will help to liberate the poor? This is a good biblical option with historical precedent, although it is not as clear as it sounds. Those who make this choice will inexorably find themselves in dissent from many of the church hierarchy with all the internal ecclesiastical disputes involved. The commitment to struggle for the rights of the people creates this situation of crisis for the church, but it can be a creative crisis, and is one which ought not to be suppressed.

Case Study Three: a Church Faces Emergency

In mid-March 1977, India voted in a free election to end the rule of the Congress Party and its leader, Mrs Indira Gandhi, and at the same time to terminate the state of emergency which had been in force for the previous 19 months. The strength of the opposition to the Congress Party surprised almost all commentators, and in their post-election summaries it was concluded that the election was a vote for freedom and a vote against the excesses of emergency.[27] The sweeping election victory followed by a peaceful transition of power is without parallel in modern Asian history, and has significance for our study of human rights.

It was partly evident during the emergency, and has been substantiated subsequently, that there were many gross violations of the people's rights during emergency rule. These may be summarized as follows:

1. There was a considerable number of political prisoners. The detention laws under the Maintenance of Internal Security Act were rigorously applied, and any person could be arrested without charge and detained without trial indefinitely. Many spent the whole period of the emergency in prison, including several political opponents of Mrs Gandhi.

2. There were documented cases of torture. Some suffered permanent physical damage, including Lawrence Fernandes, brother of labour leader George Fernandes, and Miss Snehalatha Reddy, the film star, who subsequently died as a result of the indignities she suffered.[28] Prisoners were killed by over-zealous guards.[29]

3. Urban renewal programmes systematically uprooted slum areas in Delhi, Bombay and Calcutta and the occupants were

driven outside the city limits beyond their places of work. There was no negotiation with the people, even though in some cases, such as Janata Colony in Bombay, there had been an official promise to negotiate.

4. Press censorship was total and newspapers were unable to publish criticism of either the ruling party or the effects of the emergency. Samchar, the official news agency, produced only one side of the news, as did All India Radio. Even church magazines were under censorship.

5. The right to dissent was denied. Those who wished to speak or act against any of the government policies were effectively denied the opportunity or did so at risk to themselves.

6. A programme of compulsory sterilization brought considerable suffering, especially among the poorer communities. While Mrs Gandhi herself had said that compulsory sterilization "is too drastic",[30] yet it was encouraged to flourish in many states, threatening to deny human dignity and the sanctity of human life.

We do not need to dwell on these several instances of denial of human rights. They are common enough to every country under authoritarian rule. Those who favour such centralized control will say that they recognize the harshness of such measures but this has to be balanced against the good that is done in the society, such as the improvement of conditions for the poor; increased efficiency of commerce and industry; stability of the society; and more effective centralized planning. The correlation between sets of rights is a basic question for all developing nations.

In this case study we discuss the role of the Christian church during the period of emergency to see if there are lessons for the Christian community as a whole. As background material, the Christian Institute for the Study of Religion and Society has published an omnibus collection of documents produced during the emergency, including all the major official church statements made in the 19-month period, and exchanges of correspondence and personal statements. The editorial claims that there were three basic responses by the church:

> First a group which approved the emergency either because of a minority community's loyalty to the Congress and Indira Gandhi or because of their conviction that freedom has already become a hindrance to economic development and social justice in India. A second group recognized the value of the emergency as a temporary

measure to bring much-needed discipline and welfare to the weaker sections of the people, but who felt restless at the severity of the measures of press censorship and detention without trial and other abuses. A third group was opposed to the emergency from the very beginning because of their conviction that freedom is a God-given inalienable right of man as man, and that where freedom is denied, the awakening of the masses into a self-conscious people will be halted, minimizing participation of the people in their own development, jeopardizing justice itself and turning state into tyranny.[31]

Three incidents in these 19 months indicate the depth of the split in the church: the 20-point programme of Mrs Gandhi, the fund for detenues'[32] families, and the attitude of churches to international ecumenical bodies.

THE 20-POINT ECONOMIC PROGRAMME

This programme, issued by the prime minister in July 1975, outlined the measures the government wished to adopt to assist the society's development. At the request of the Congress Party president, Shri D. K. Barooah, a letter was sent to the National Christian Council of India (NCC/I) seeking its support for the programme.[33] At the NCC/I's assembly in November 1975, this support was not given but instead the NCC/I was asked to arrange a meeting between the prime minister and church representatives to discuss the programme.[34] After eight months of attempts to reconcile some of the opposing views, the decision to meet with the prime minister was quietly deferred.[35]

Some of the church leaders, however, were optimistically promoting the 20-point programme, and one went to the extent of comparing it with the Nazareth Declaration of Jesus.[36] Dr J. Russell Chandran, Principal of United Theological College in Bangalore, had some reservations about the emergency, but no hesitation in supporting the 20-point programme:

> The Christian churches... have a special responsibility now to come out boldly and enthusiastically to give full support along with other communities, political parties and organizations for the implementation of the 20-point economic reform launched by the prime minister.[37]

This positive support was echoed by other Christian leaders, and reached its culmination when a delegation of "leaders of the Christian community" visited Mrs Gandhi on 10 February 1977, and the moderator of the Church of North India (CNI) affirmed "we consider it our bounden duty to assure you that we as a community are with you and behind you",[38] a remark which was criticized by the secular press as well as several CNI clergy.[39]

Through the official courts, churches gave support to the 20-point programme, although at its synod in 1976 the Church of South India (CSI) only did so with qualifications. The CSI resolution was the sole critical voice from the official church bodies, and it appealed to the prime minister to withdraw the restrictions on press freedom and restore fundamental rights.[40]

Those church people who eulogized the 20-point programme often held a theology in which the church should take no part in politics.[41] This is a common affirmation, especially in evangelical circles. But in giving open support to the 20-point programme they were, de facto, acting politically and helping to give an air of respectability to the emergency rule. In a state which is being directed and controlled from the centre, an endorsement of one sector of that state's programme is an indirect endorsement of the whole. C. T. Kurien, the economist, points out that "the 20-point programme is largely an attempt to legitimize the politics of the low order that the emergency represents".[42] The programme had to be seen in the context in which it was presented, and this was, at least in part, to establish legitimization for political action.

THE FUND FOR DETENUES' FAMILIES

During the emergency there was a proper concern on the part of a few church leaders for the families of detenues. Together they drafted an appeal letter and submitted it to the churches and church-related organizations.[43] The church establishment considered the request, but not one official church body gave its support. The Church of North India denied any humanitarian concern for the families of the prisoners.[44] The NCC/I did not give its endorsement, and neither did the Christian Agency for Social Action (CASA), the official church aid organization. This led Dr M. M. Thomas, one of the promoters of the fund, to state: "Why should the church exist if it repudiates all moral and human concerns in the situation?"[45]

The passivity of the Indian churches over the detenues fund is difficult to reconcile with concern for the suffering. In all of the many sensitive and potentially explosive situations related to human rights, the one area which is most understood by both governments and churches is the moral responsibility to give humanitarian aid to families of prisoners. In countries such as the Philippines and Korea, where there are similar situations, the National Council of Churches holds official funds for distribution to the families of detainees. This is an area in which the churches can act without compromise as an expression of concern for moral issues.

THE CHURCHES AND INTERNATIONAL ECUMENICAL BODIES

The international Christian community was closely following the development of events in India and on 9 October 1975 Dr Philip Potter, general secretary of the World Council of Churches, wrote to Mrs Gandhi expressing concern about detention and the restriction of freedoms.[46] Copies of this letter were sent to Indian churches and the NCC/I with a covering letter from the WCC's Commission of the Churches on International Affairs.[47] On 18 June 1976, the general secretary of the Christian Conference of Asia (CCA), Dr Yap Kim Hao, wrote to the NCC/I asking them to take some action on behalf of the political prisoners,[48] and this was followed, on 19 July 1976, with a further letter from the CCIA asking for all member churches to send greetings to the Indian government on its 29th anniversary of independence (15 August 1976), and requesting the release of the political prisoners.[49]

The earlier letter received no official response, but the letters of June and July 1976 led to two major resolutions, one from the NCC/I executive, and one from the CNI executive. The NCC/I response is summarized as follows:

> The WCC should not ask for action in any country without first consulting the constituent bodies in that country. The WCC and CCA do not understand the Indian issues. Western liberal democracies and the western news media have an anti-India attitude. The Indian churches are mature enough to handle this matter on their own.[50]

The CNI passed a series of resolutions which it then forwarded to Mrs Gandhi. After expressing gratitude and appreciation for her dynamic leadership, they address the overseas agencies:

> The CNI does not sympathize with the views expressed by these councils on the Indian situation by assuming, unsolicited, the role of champions of Indian freedom and would not desire the WCC/CCA to make public statements and comments resulting in a false,

> distorted picture of India with which the CNI would not agree and which is most embarrassing to the people of the land who have rallied round the present leadership and are determined to support the programmes of the government of India...[51]

The practical question which emerges is whether international bodies should make statements or initiate action concerning a national situation without first consulting the national churches. It is, of course, a basic axiom of international ecumenical bodies that they must relate as closely as possible to their national constituents, and this is the whole basis of staff visits, exchange of correspondence, conferences and assemblies. To be effective, the international body needs to have communication at several levels: that is, not only with official church courts, but also with people at the grassroots, sodalities of different kinds, and locally-based agencies.

But when the international agencies have discussed with national and local people and weighed up the information received, they have not only a right but also a responsibility to speak to a situation in whatever seems to be the appropriate manner. This must be the *modus vivendi* of international organizations, and no concession should be made on this point. Indeed, there are compelling reasons for this. A fundamental reality of an authoritarian situation is that access to news is denied to the nation's people, who consequently do not have the resources with which to make an objective or responsible decision. The whole dynamic of an authoritarian regime is that the people within the country are in ignorance of the facts about their own nation. This adds to the responsibility of external groups to make some comment on the basis of wider knowledge.

The second rationale for international bodies taking action, either by a statement or in some other way, is that there are groups within the authoritarian state who need the support this action gives. The knowledge that international organizations keep raising human rights questions is of crucial consequence for those who are the victims of violations, for such solidarity sustains hope and is often the only encouragement.

Thirdly, there is the strong theological reason that the church is, in essence, intention, and constitution, an international fellowship which crosses national boundaries. Churches must not fall into the secular trap of venerating the nation-state, but must recognize that the bounds of the church go beyond "Jew and Greek" and other national distinctions (Gal. 3 : 28). The church in Germany, for example, must speak to the church in India, and the Indian church to the German church. This mutual witness and response must not be silenced, or an integral part of the church will be lost.

For international agencies, the question of which voice to hear — the voice of the official church bodies or the (often conflicting) voices of other Christian sodalities — is an agonizing decision. There is anxiety not to aggravate the situation of the oppressed, but the equal desire not to let a dehumanizing situation be accorded the approval of silence. This means that serious study, including political and structural analysis, must precede any public utterance.

International ecumenical bodies could not accept the stance of the NCC/I and at the same time retain their integrity. To do so would mean silent acquiescence in the face of racism in Southern Africa, genocide in Cambodia, and in many other unjust and inhuman situations. For international ecumenical bodies there is a moral imperative to make some kind of open response to matters of injustice, with or without the support of the people within the nation concerned.

A thorough post mortem on the Indian events will be instructive for the church's stance in a situation where human rights are being denied. This must not be done in a judgmental sense, certainly not by persons who are not directly involved. From within India there are signs that some categorical questions are already being asked about the church's role during the emergency. Some have been openly critical, such as C. T. Kurien who summarizes: "On the whole, the lead given by church dignitaries was a shameful display of docility, naïveté and opportunism." [52] The official magazine of the National Christian Council is more subdued, but critical:

> Except for a few small protest and prophetic groups and individuals, the church in India on the whole was a silent spectator of historic events. It will be quite a task to establish our credibility with the new government.[53]

To struggle for justice and to affirm human dignity is the mission of the church. Failure at this point has wider, more universal significance than just at that moment in history. For this reason, the Indian experience speaks to us all.

44

NOTES

1 Of the major mission-field nations, Japan and Thailand both have less than 1% of Christians in the total population.

2 Kim Yong Bok: "Reflections on People's Rights in Asia." Paper presented to Asia Youth Mission, Lantau Island, Hong Kong, 11 May 1977 (mimeographed).

3 Nigel Cameron: *From Bondage to Liberation: East Asia 1860-1952*. Hong Kong: Oxford University Press, 1975, p. 157.

4 R. C. Allen: *Korea's Sygman Rhee*. Tokyo: Tuttle, 1960.

5 "Korea." In *Encyclopaedia Britannica*, 15th ed., 1975, Macropaedia 10, p. 511.

6 "Declaration for Democratic National Salvation", 1 March 1976. At least three English-language translations of the Declaration have been made (mimeographed).

7 "Theological Declaration of Korean Christians", 20 May 1973. In *Documents on the Struggle for Democracy in Korea*, Emergency Christian Conference on Korean Problems. Tokyo: Shinkyo Shuppansha, 1975, pp. 37-43.

8 "Statement of Seoul District Prosecutor's Office", issued 10 March 1976, by Suh Chung Gak, Chief Prosecutor. Names of those indicted revised 26 March 1976 (both mimeographed).

9 "Park Asked to Free Dissidents", statement of Seoul Embassy in Tokyo. *Mainichi Daily News*, Tokyo, 8 March 1976.

10 Notes on the trial were taken in Korean and transcribed. The most comprehensive selection appears in *Korea Communique*, Tokyo, John M. Nakajima ed., "Japan Emergency Christian Conference on Korean Problems." No. 1, 2 August 1976, pp. 1-15; No. 2, 10 September 1976, pp. 1-10; No. 3, 10 October 1976, p. 3. Other verbatim reports were printed in *Newsweek*, 2 August 1976, and the *Far Eastern Economic Review*, Hong Kong, 21 May 1976, and on mimeographed sheets. The summary here is the author's.

11 "Our View" or "Our Position." Seoul: Korean National Council of Churches, 26 March 1976 (mimeographed).

12 "Statement of the Bishops of Korea." In *Information on Human Development*. Manila: Office for Human Development, 1 May 1976, p. 3.

13 "Our View", *op. cit.*, and "Conference on the Social Responsibility of Christians", 13-14 May 1976. Seoul: Ewha University (mimeographed).

14 Hahm Suk Hon: "Letter to Friends Around the World." *Korea Communique*, Tokyo, No. 2, 10 September 1976, p. 10.

15 Alison M. O'Grady: "The Women Wore Purple Crosses." *Church Labour Letter*, Doshisha University, Kyoto, No. 136, 1976, pp. 1-3.

16 Bernard Wideman: "Before the Altar of Protest." *Far Eastern Economic Review*, Hong Kong, 10 January 1975, p. 12.

17 Ferdinand E. Marcos: *The Democratic Revolution in the Philippines*. New Jersey: Prentice Hall, 1974, p. 21.

18 *Ibid.*, p. 22.

19 Gustavo Gutierrez: *Theology of Liberation*. New York: Orbis, 1975. The Philippine edition is called *The New Man*. Manila: CBI Books, 1973.

20 Edicio de la Torre: "The Christian Participation in the Struggle for Liberation" (mimeographed). Also "The Passion, Death and Resurrection of the Petty Bourgeois Christian". *An Asian Theology of Liberation: the Philippines*, No. 5 in the series "The Future of the Missionary Enterprise." Rome: IDOC, 1973, pp. 22-26. — "Persecution always Strengthens Christians." Interview with Ed de la Torre. *Liberation*, Manila, Vol. II, No. 7, 10 December 1973, and "The Filipino Christian: Guidelines and Proper Response." Ateneo Lecture Series in *Manggugubat*. College of Forestry, U.P. College Laguna, Vol. 4, April-June 1972, pp. 5-8. The latter two texts in Simeon G. Del Rosario: *The Church and State Today*. Quezon City: Manlapaz Publishing, 1975, pp. 27-32, 74-78.

21 Association of Major Religious Superiors in the Philippines. *Various Reports* (mimeographed), 5 January 1975, pp. 21 f.

22 Fr Louis Jalandoni: "Persecution Always Strengthens Christians." *Liberation*, Manila, Vol. II, No. 7, 10 December 1973. In Simeon G. Del Rosario, *op. cit.*, p. 76.

23 Camilo Torres: Statement of 24 June 1965. In *The Church and Revolution*, eds François Houtart and André Rousseau. New York: Orbis, 1971, p. 200.

24 Fr Restituto Lumanlan, provincial consultor, Divine Word Missionaries: "Statement of Concern for all Political Prisoners." Manila, December 1973 (mimeographed).

25 Association of Major Religious Superiors: (Men) Fr Lope Castillo, (Women) Sr Christine Tan: "Concern for Justice." Manila, 21 December 1974 (printed sheet).

26 Archbishop Teopiso Alberto of Nueva Caceres: "On Sovereignty and the Church." Speech at Malacanang, Manila, 26 January 1975. In Simeon G. Del Rosario, *op. cit.*, p. 86.

27 Emergency excesses were cited by the Congress Party as one of the reasons for their defeat. A. Hariharan: "Congress Counts the Cost." *Far Eastern Economic Review*, 6 May 1977, p. 31.

28 Snehalatha Reddy: *A Prison Diary*. Karnataka: Human Rights Committee, 1977.

29 Bombay Clergy: "Voice of Conscience." In "Christians and the Emergency: Some Documents." *Religion and Society*, Christian Institute for the Study of Religion and Society, Bangalore, Vol. XXII, Nos 2 and 3, June and September 1977, p. 82.

30 Catholic Union of India: "Memorandum Sent to the Prime Minister on Compulsory Sterilization", 13 March 1976. In "Christians and the Emergency", *op. cit.*, p. 99.

31 Editorial, "Christians and the Emergency", *op. cit.*, p. 1.

32 The word "detenues" is used in India to refer to political prisoners. So far as we know, it is not used in other countries in this form.

33 M. A. Z. Rolston: "Letter to Heads of Churches in India", New Delhi, 1 August 1975. In "Christians and the Emergency", *op. cit.*, pp. 22-23.

34 Minutes of the Fifteenth Assembly of the National Christian Council of India, 75 : 64, pp. 42-43. In "Christians and the Emergency", *op. cit.*, p. 26.

[35] Minutes of Meeting of Heads of Churches or their Representatives, Madras, 13 July 1976. In "Christians and the Emergency", *op. cit.*, p. 37.

[36] *North India Churchman*, Delhi, December 1976. Quoted by M. M. Thomas in "Christians and the Emergency", *op. cit.*, p. 256.

[37] J. R. Chandran: "Getting the Priorities Right." *The Guardian*, Madras, 14 August 1975. In "Christians and the Emergency", *op. cit.*, p. 141.

[38] "Christians Back Indira." *The Times of India*, 11 February 1977. In "Christians and the Emergency", *op. cit.*, pp. 75-76.

[39] Mark Sunder Rao: "Comment." *The Guardian*, Madras, 15 February 1977 — Canon Subir Biswas: letter to *Statesman*, Calcutta, 26 February 1977 — Consultation of Bombay Clergy and Laity, 24-26 February 1977 — CISRS Consultation, February 1977. All quotes in "Christians and the Emergency", *op. cit.*, pp. 77-80.

[40] Church of South India: "Resolution of the Fifteenth Synod", 13-17 June 1976. In "Christians and the Emergency", *op. cit.*, p. 44.

[41] "We do not involve the church in politics of the time... Our position is to stand on the side... We are neutral." Bishop of Calcutta, interview with group of Asian church leaders, 20 August 1977.

[42] C. T. Kurien: Personal correspondence with J. R. Chandran, Madras, 12 March 1976. In "Christians and the Emergency", *op. cit.*, p. 108.

[43] Detenues Family Distress Relief Fund, 10 May 1976. In "Christians and the Emergency", *op. cit.*, p. 80. This fund collected over Rs 40,000 and gave monthly aid to about 40 families.

[44] M. M. Thomas: "Religion and Society: Newsletter No. 7." Tiruvalla, 24 December 1976. In "Christians and the Emergency", *op. cit.*, p. 256.

[45] *Ibid.*, p. 256.

[46] Philip Potter: "Letter to Prime Minister Mrs Indira Gandhi", 9 October 1975. In "Christians and the Emergency", *op. cit.*, p. 3.

[47] Leopoldo J. Niilus: "Letter to Member Churches of the WCC in India", 22 October 1975. In "Christians and the Emergency", *op. cit.*, pp. 4-7.

[48] Yap Kim Hao: "Letter to NCC/I", 18 June 1976. In "Christians and the Emergency", *op. cit.*, p. 8.

[49] Leopoldo J. Niilus: "Circular letter to Member Churches and Councils of the WCC", 19 July 1976. In "Christians and the Emergency", *op. cit.*, pp. 9-10.

[50] Mathai Zachariah: "Letter to the Christian Conference of Asia and the Churches' Commission on International Affairs, WCC", 1 December 1976. In "Christians and the Emergency", *op. cit.*, pp. 39-40. Summary by the author.

[51] A. C. Dharmaraj: "Letter to Prime Minister Shrinathi Indira Gandhi", 21 September 1976. In "Christians and the Emergency", *op. cit.*, pp. 47-49.

[52] C. T. Kurien: "Indian Elections: an Interpretation." Unpublished paper, 23 March 1977.

[53] Mathai Zachariah, "The New Day in India." *NCC Review*, Nagpur, May 1977.

IV. The contemporary debate on human rights

> *"The process whereby the people themselves regain the humanity they have lost through oppression leads to an explosive turning point; the people experience a sudden and expansive awakening and the miracle of a leap in history is seen."* [1]

Behind our concern for the rights of the people lies that moment which imprisoned Korean poet Kim Chi Ha calls the "sudden and expansive awakening". It is this moment in time when an oppressive society is broken open and the people discover their dignity and their sense of destiny. Such events are rare in the history of each nation: the coming of peace after war; the end of colonial rule; a sweeping election victory; the death or overthrow of a dictator; an exodus from bondage. The sense of national euphoria and the long sigh of relief which follow these events are the voices of the people who have found their liberation.

Although it is through these penultimate moments in history that we understand human dignity and destiny, life is not lived on that plane for very long. Most of our human experience takes place at the more mundane level of the smaller bondages and restrictions under which we labour in daily routines. This is why catalogues of rights are required: to provide a criteria by which we can gauge the tendencies towards the human which are either inherent in, or absent from, any particular society. From such frameworks national constitutions and laws are written, and it is to them that the oppressed can appeal.

Whatever these affirmations say, we cannot be blind to the fact that they will be interpreted politically. The national leaders who implement the human rights statements start their reasoning from a political ideology and not from an abstract philosophy of humanity. Our discussion on the current human rights debate must be sensitive to this political reality.

Human rights as seen by major power blocs [2]

The historical survey in chapter II showed some of the political upheavals which have helped to shape our various attitudes to human rights. Those whose educational conditioning followed

48

the teaching of western liberalism will have a different interpretation of an event from those who came through the Marxist revolutions of eastern Europe, and these in turn will both differ from the understanding of developing nations.

In this section three principal categories will be used to show how human interpretation is influenced by ideological factors. As a convenient shorthand we will adopt the three "worlds" of journalists.[3] The western capitalist societies centred mainly in western Europe and North America but including Japan, Australia and New Zealand constitute the First World; communist-socialist societies following the Marxist-Leninist model are the Second World; and those non-aligned developing nations which do not belong to either of the power blocs can be described as the Third World. Inevitably, this division is an over-simplification and does not allow for the great differences within each bloc. However, it provides a sufficient basis for an analysis of the differing expectations and interpretations of human rights questions.

1. THE FIRST WORLD

a) *Self-understanding:* The capitalist world sees itself as the defender of liberty and upholder of rights and democracy. The declarations of the French and American Revolutions have profoundly affected the historic processes in western civilization, and have been a rallying point at moments of national and international crisis. The US president's emphasis on human rights is entirely consistent with western capitalist history. Particular stress is laid on individual liberties, which are protected by constitutions and a liberal interpretation of the rule of law. The right to hold and express minority views, to possess property, to have a fair trial before one's peers, to have freedom of expression in public media, and the rights of fair electoral procedures are all jealously guarded within the First World. The First World played the dominant role in formulating the "Universal Declaration of Human Rights". It claims to uphold these rights more adequately than other nations and, therefore, cherishes the title of "a free society".

b) *The First World understanding of the Second World:* Since the communist revolutions have not had the full approval of the majority, the people are repressed and denied their rights under communism. Communist rule is dictatorial, and the single party state denies the possibility of dissent, if necessary by forceful repression. The refusal to allow self-determination in Hungary, Czechoslovakia and Tibet are instances of the repression of people's movements for the sake of ideology. The refusal to allow political dissent has led to imprisonment, torture, exile, brainwashing, character defamation and forced confessions. The West sees the flow of refugees seeking asylum in the West as proof that communist society is repressive of human dignity. The denial of freedom of movement, freedom of expression, and a proper electoral process is further evidence of this. First World churches reflect their national ethos. There is the belief that both European communism and Maoism are inimical to Christianity, and deliberately restrict religious freedom. The inference is sometimes drawn that those churches which survive in eastern Europe have done so by compromising their beliefs — a view which is encouraged by refugees.

c) *The First World understanding of the Third World:* There is ambivalence in the western understanding of the Third World nations, because there are extensive historical links as well as the ever-present desire to retain western influence over the non-aligned nations lest they become communist. Even so, the liberal conscience of the West is angered by some blatant human rights violations in nations such as Haiti, Uganda, Chile, South Korea or Rwanda. Most international human rights organizations, for example, Amnesty International and the International Commission of Jurists, have their base in the western bloc and there is widespread popular support for their criticisms of third world excesses. Since a number of third world nations are important trading partners or sources of raw materials, the protest at government level is often muted.

2. The Second World

a) *Self-understanding:* The communist revolutions saw themselves as part of the historically determined process for restoring the rights to the people. After years of capitalist and bourgeois rule by persons whose motivation was their own self-interest, the communist revolutions gave back to the people the power to determine their own future. Competition gave way to cooperation, and the rights of rulers yielded to the rights of the masses. This gives communist states a sense of historical mission as the fore-runners of the new world society. This new society will preserve the community rights and spell the end of the competitive systems of private enterprise. Rights belong to the whole society and not just to individuals. If individuals threaten the well-being of the wider community they must be punished. Basic human rights are better protected under communism than under any other form of government.

b) *Second World understanding of the First World:* The First World speaks about human rights in a self-righteous manner, but in fact is the principal offender. Western democracy denies people their rights in both subtle and blatant ways. The competitive system concentrates capital and leads to inefficiency, wastage of natural resources, unfair trade practices, and money manipulation, and the net results include poverty and unemployment. (There were eight million unemployed in the United States and one million in Britain at the beginning of 1977.[4]) Alienation is the fundamental contradiction in capitalist society. It occurs through the ownership of property, which in turn gives rise to a non-productive elite. Loneliness and disenchantment mark the youth of western society, and corruption in high places indicates a basically unjust system. The official Czechoslovakian newspaper claims: "It is the capitalist states which are shamelessly trampling on human rights."[5] Christian groups in eastern Europe are defensive about western church criticism of their role. In response to the popular western question: "Can a Christian be a communist?", the East European will reply: "Can a Christian be a capitalist?" Western society is often portrayed as a society which has become consumer-oriented and materialistic to the exclusion of the Christian virtues of compassion and community.

c) *The Second World understanding of the Third World:* Communism is selective in condemning Third World nations. Like the First World, the Second World will assiduously study the political implications and possible political gain from making a strong stand relating to rights. If a criticism is made, the background portentous presence of the western world is castigated. Communists see many third world nations as puppet governments, kept in power by American aid and armaments. If the rulers become oppressive, this will be interpreted as a way of retaining power for the capitalist system. The non-aligned nations are to be encouraged to take part in the world Soviet revolution. Maoism sees itself as identified more closely with third world nations and, therefore, is slower to be critical in instances of rights violations. In its battle with the USSR over hegemony in the communist world, China is more likely to use third world disturbances as an arena to fight this larger ideological difference.

3. THE THIRD WORLD

a) *Self-understanding*: The Third World, especially in Africa and Asia, is conscious of its difference from either the First or the Second World. Much of its cultural heritage dates back centuries, and has developed independently of the Graeco-Roman traditions of the West. While there are some similarities in the third world understanding of the human, yet it did not develop the competitive individualism which marked the 19th and 20th centuries in western Christian nations. When a third world nation is questioned about its actions in regard to human rights, the rulers will often return to their traditional history and claim, for example, that they are seeking African answers, or an Asian-style democracy. It will sometimes be claimed that the people understand an assertive leadership better than western-style freedoms. The intense concern for economic development is over-riding. Third world leaders who recognize that they are taking unpopular and stern measures will justify the stand by claiming that some lesser rights must be sacrificed in order to achieve economic growth.

b) *The Third World understanding of the First World:* Third world nations are irritated by first world accusations of human rights violations, because they claim that the First World has violated the basic rights of developing nations for centuries. They look back to the exploitation of the colonialist era as the root of many of their current economic ills, and recognize that the heavy industrialization of the capitalist nations has given an economic lever through which they can control a large sector of the world's economy for their own profit. Through multinational corporations and the control of capital flow, the western nations have a stranglehold on third world economy.

The Third World reacts strongly when it is criticized for the same things which take place in the First World. They claim that a western society which can produce a Watergate and industrial bribery is in no position to criticize corruption in third world nations. Since the struggle to survive is so intense in poorer countries, they are angered when western nations appear to be more concerned about free trial than about basic rights to food and shelter. There is the suspicion that the capitalist nations use their intelligence services and their economic strength to keep the third world nations in a continual state of poverty and, therefore, dependence. This can be rationalized by criticisms about human rights violations.

c) *Third World attitudes to the Second World:* One of the human rights advocated by third world nations is the right of a people to self-determination. At times communism, both in Europe and Asia, has aroused the anger of third world nations for its influence on, and support for, revolutionary groups within the borders of an independent nation. This is seen as a violation of national sovereignty and independence. To many third world nations the communist bloc is considered to be just as exploitative as western capitalism. They have seen the same desire to purchase natural resources and convert them to manufactured goods which sell at prices no less than those of the capitalist nations. Communism is seen as a form of state capitalism which generates just as much injustice as private capitalism.

* * *

This summary makes no pretence of being exhaustive, and does not allow for subtleties within each outline. What it does highlight, however, is that for each human rights violation situation there are many possible positions, each based on a fundamental political stance. Each nation will read a human rights violation through its own ideologically-tinted glasses. It is this reality which makes the rational and objective assessment of human rights a political impossibility. The fact that a nation has ratified the "Universal Declaration of Human Rights", and even written it into its constitution, provides no guarantee that it will interpret it in the same way as other nations.

Ultimately, the political leaders of each nation are motivated by national self-interest, economic development and political survival. It is necessary for them to retain credibility in order to survive, and therefore their affirmations on human rights always sound altruistic and impressive. Yet these public affirmations have little practical meaning. Decisions on human rights will be made finally in line with major ideological alliances and possible spheres of influence, and we must be realistic about the limited room for movement this gives to political leadership. At the same time, governments are vulnerable to pressure, provided the goal does not deviate too greatly from their own image of their role.

Current American policy

The emergence of human rights as a central issue in international politics since 1976 has been due to the strong predication of the theme by US president Mr Jimmy Carter. This has required some further interpretation, and in April 1977 the American secretary of state gave a major policy speech on the American understanding of human rights. He claimed that human rights are to be understood in three ways:

> ... The right to be free from governmental violation of the integrity of the person. Such violations include torture; cruel, inhumane or degrading treatment or punishment; and arbitrary arrest or imprisonment. And they include denial of the right to a fair trial and invasion of the home.
> ... The right to the fulfillment of such vital needs as food, shelter, health care and education. We recognize that the fulfillment of this right will depend, in part, on the stage of a nation's economic development. But we also know that this right can be violated by a government's action or inaction — for example, through corrupt official processes which divert resources to an elite at the expense of the needy, or through indifference to the plight of the poor.
> ... The right to enjoy civil and political liberties: freedom of thought; of religion; of assembly; freedom of speech; freedom of the press; freedom of movement both within and outside one's own country; freedom to take part in government.[6]

Predictably, the American statement breaks no new ground. It is a restatement of the classical American position, phrased in the liberal tradition, with strong emphasis on personal liberties, although the actual language is carefully modulated so that "individualism" is not visibly mentioned. Small changes may be significant. Mr Vance has placed the economic and social rights ahead of the political and civil liberties, and this reversal of the usual order of western affirmation may be a recognition of the poor countries' anger about western priorities. Also significant is that the list of economic and social rights does not include the right to work, a point at which western society is especially vulnerable and one which is often mentioned by Soviet leaders.

The new American political initiative has been welcomed in many places, and for a variety of often contradictory reasons.[7]

In the United States, extensive support comes from such hetero-
geneous groups as those who want to attack the Russians and
those with a sentimental humanitarianism. In countries under
oppressive rule, the American emphasis has been seized upon by
those who are the victims of society as a way of getting American
political leverage to help their cause. Political leaders in most
countries have made a more cautious response. While acknow-
ledging that there will be some positive benefits from the American
initiative, there are good reasons to be apprehensive about its
long-term effect. There are enough equivocal aspects to the politicizing of human rights to raise three main reservations.

ARROGANCE, MESSIANIC PASSION AND POLITICIZING

There is, firstly, an implied arrogance and even moral hypocrisy
about any single nation raising the human rights question in
relation to any other nation. No country speaks in this area
with a clear conscience because none is in such a state of grace
that it cannot be faulted for human rights violations.

If we analyse the American stand more carefully, and especially
the way the United States has acted towards overseas violations,
we recognize a bias in favour of civil and political liberties. In
this area the Americans have developed a legal and political system which has many notable achievements for human liberty.
Although there are times when this demand for personal liberty
has gone to excess, it has been able to give ordinary people protection from some of the indiscriminate denials of liberty which
are found in other nations. If the criteria for human rights is the
number of political prisoners or the amount of freedom to publish
or to possess a firearm, then one ends with the conclusion of the
Asian Wall Street Journal: "There is a connection between respect
for human rights and political democracy."[8]

But human rights do not begin and end with these political and
civil rights. Also involved are the economic, social and cultural
rights of the people, and at this point, by moral or by Christian
criteria, the record of the United States does not stand close
scrutiny. To hear the black American tell it is to hear a different
story about freedom in American society:

> Here in Mississippi I knew the racism that takes away human
> rights. Here I knew oppression as a child, being without a father
> or mother and living in a family of sharecroppers, working for
> nothing.[9]

The extent of poverty, unemployment, racism and discrimination is visibly evident in the United States, and means that the democratic dream is not universally realized. The denials are subtle but no less real for, as Daniel Berrigan once said, western history has a tendency to liberate man in public and precious areas, but to progressively enslave him in more mysterious ways.

The second reservation about the new American stance is that it is suggestive of the messianic passion to save the world which has tended to keep recurring in American politics. President William McKinley, in 1901, explained his decision to occupy the Philippines as the result of divine guidance "to uplift and civilize and Christianize them".[10] Similar motivations led Wilson to punish the Mexicans and recent presidents to support unpopular regimes in Vietnam.

The dilemma facing many other nations is that they do not see human rights in the simplistic context of democracy. President Kennedy understood a little of this subtlety when he said that, instead of making the world safe for democracy, "we (America) ought to be attempting to make the world safe for diversity".[11] This view has more political realism within it and avoids the danger of any one nation setting itself up as the arbiter of what constitutes human rights violations. At the present stage of international politics there is not the slightest hope that "offending" nations will recognize or respect American overt acts on behalf of human rights. To publicly attack the Soviet Union on human rights, for example, is intolerable for the Russians since it strikes at the very integrity of the whole Soviet system. The basis of the Russian revolution and of their subsequent history reflects a view of history and of the people's economic and civil rights which begins from a fundamentally different *zeitgeist* to that of democracy.

Nor will third world nations accept a rationale about human rights which comes from one of the most prosperous nations of the world. They will ask the question of prime minister Lee Kwan Yew of Singapore: "Can we and must we all accept the same moral standards?"[12] And General Kriangsak of Thailand puts his country's case by saying that it is essential (for the United States) to take into account "the different processes of civilization through which other people have to go" as well as "the stage of development and the personal characteristics of the society concerned".[13]

None of these objections should dissuade us from the search for acceptable international standards of human behaviour and respect for the rights of all people. However, they do suggest that our attempts must be genuinely international, and that no one nation can abrogate to itself the right of unilateral action. Any charges brought by the Americans against other nations have elements of truth within them, but so also do the counter-charges.

This leads us to the final reservation about the current debate: that there is a danger of politicizing a situation which is certainly political, but which can only be understood as an apolitical allegory. That is to say, human rights should only enter a nation's political policies as part of a broader-based supra-political conviction. Intervention must come from an affirmation about the human and go beyond our national interpretations or any single political ideology.

If this is not continually affirmed, then we will lose human rights as a valuable and universally understood tool for human welfare and it will become yet another part of the verbal political posturing of one nation against another.

NOTES

1 Kim Chi Ha: "Declaration of Conscience", smuggled from West Gate prison, Seoul, Korea, 8 August 1975. Trans. *AMPO*, the Japan-Asia Quarterly Review, Tokyo, Vol. 7, No. 3, July-September 1975, p. 41.

2 An adaptation of the text in this section, prepared by the author, appeared in *One World*, the monthly magazine of the WCC, Geneva, October 1977.

3 Mao tse Tung has proposed an alternative "Three-Worlds" theory which places Russia and the USA together and secondary economic powers in the Second World. China then joins poorer nations as the Third World. While more true to the GNP this division is less helpful for ideological analysis.

4 Hella Pick: "West Violates Human Rights." *The Guardian Weekly*, Manchester, UK, 20 February 1977.

5 *Ibid.*

6 Cyrus Vance: "Speech to the University of Georgia." *Washington Post*, 1 May 1977, and *The Guardian*, Manchester, UK, 8 May 1977.

7 Charles W. Yost: "How the US Harms Human Rights Policy." *Christian Science Monitor*, Boston, 26 August 1977, p. 31.

8 Peter Berger: "Connecting Capitalism, Democracy, Human Rights." *Asian Wall Street Journal*, Hong Kong, 2 August 1977, p. 4.

9 John Perkins: "What It Means to be the Church." *International Review of Mission*, WCC, Vol. LXVI, No. 263, July 1977, p. 244.

10 Pat Holt: "Too Much Zeal on Human Rights." *Christian Science Monitor*, Boston, 3 August 1977, p. 15.

11 *Ibid.*, p. 15.

12 Lee, Kwan Yew, *Straits Times*, Singapore, 6 May 1977, p. 1.

13 General Kriangsak Chamanand: "What Price Human Rights?" *Far Eastern Economic Review*, Hong Kong, 22 July 1977, p. 14.

V. A human rights prognosis

"The credibility gap in human rights" is a phrase coined by Mr Sean McBride who was, at the time, secretary general of the International Commission of Jurists.[1] It referred to the gap between the standards which governments proclaim and the reality of their practice in enforcing or suppressing these rights, and it brings us to consider the ways by which the world community can move towards a more rational promotion of the people's rights.

One automatically begins any discussion of this kind by looking towards the United Nations with expectancy. The "Universal Declaration of Human Rights" is certainly one of the significant statements of this century; after allowing for the possibility of bias on the part of the drafters, it still remains the most widely accepted affirmation about the rights of people, and this acceptance goes across all the usual political divisions between nations. But getting agreement on a form of words is only a partial step, and the United Nations itself recognized that it must find the means for implementation. The covenants were one attempt to do this, and the establishment of a Human Rights Commission is another. A new proposal promoted in the UN is the appointment of a High Commissioner for Human Rights.[2] So far all of these measures fall far short of the people's expectations.

Each year the United Nations receives approximately 20,000 petitions detailing human rights violations.[3] Almost all disappear into the limbo of the organization. Hundreds of cases are considered each year by the Sub-Commission on the Prevention of Discrimination and the Protection of Minorities, and in 1968 it finally concluded that there was a "consistent pattern of gross violations" in Haiti and Greece, but took no action. Again, in 1973 the Sub-Commission approved eight human rights cases and forwarded them to the Commission on Human Rights. In closed session, the Commission set up a five-member working group to consider the eight cases and any subsequent items referring to them. By 1975 no action had followed on the eight cases, nor on an additional two which had been forwarded. By 1976 these "gross violations of human rights" had disappeared from the agenda.[3] Ivor Richards of Britain described the process as a paper facade for "camouflaging reality".[3]

It is easy to be cynical about such failures, but the United Nations has not been as completely impotent as these facts would suggest. In areas of racism, for example, it has achieved some success in focusing attention on the apartheid system in the Republic of South Africa, as well as on other instances of racism. But this is one area of human rights which is understood by the majority of the voting delegates at UN assemblies. Most other areas pose an indirect threat to a majority of the member states and are, therefore, not open to direct exposure, and the machinery for genuine implementation would not be approved by the General Assembly.

The implementation of human rights

So long as the nation states control their own rule of law, their own defence and security arrangements, and determine their own economic system, we cannot look to an international arbiter such as the United Nations to make definitive and enforceable rules to govern their actions in these critical areas. The possibility of any nation handing over judicial, security or economic decisions to an international body is inconceivable at the present stage of human development. The nation state is sacred, and all treaties and declarations bow to this god. Even the good word of the "Universal Declaration of Human Rights" is rendered sterile by the "domestic jurisdiction" clause of the charter.

When President Marcos of the Philippines was questioned about the way in which the Philippines had violated civil and political rights (through suspension of the electoral process and habeus corpus, prison without trial and suspected cases of torture), he replied that the Philippines had faithfully kept the charter and observed political rights, adding: "The 'Universal Declaration of Human Rights' specifically states that wherever there is an emergency these rights may be suspended for a while."[4] As a lawyer, President Marcos knew that the nations who make up the UN would continue to uphold the principle of non-interference in national affairs, and that the "domestic jurisdiction" clause gave each nation the protection and privilege it needed in order to protect its own interests. No nation will hand over to others the control of its own future.

It raises false expectations to look to the United Nations as a panacea for the world's human rights violations, and we have already outlined the equally false hope of any single nation becoming the determiner of the world's morals. So long as the inviolability of the nation state is retained, the solution must be found within the nation itself. Political realism at this point is essential. The past 20 years have been replete with examples of nations that perpetrated acts which were morally outrageous by almost any definition of human rights. Yet the world has watched acts of genocide, torture and indiscriminate violence and been unable to intervene. Even when international outrage has been nearly unanimous — as in the case of the illegal regime in Rhodesia — the strongest possible action in the form of economic sanctions has not been able to change the direction of the country's internal policies.

Despite a growing internationalism in some visible areas of public life, there is a corresponding growth of a new form of tough nationalism. This has come about through the development of technocratic states which concentrate their power in a small elite, and retain that power by the use of economic and military measures. The genesis of this political development could be dated to 1964 when "Brazil opened the new era by setting up a government prototype, a new state whose aim it was to create a new society based on the national security system".[5] Such states are not fascist in the historical sense, since they do not necessarily hold the allegiance of the bulk of the people, but their power base is in the use of technocracy, a fact which led Dr Herb Feith to use the description "techno-fascism"[6], because it highlights the respect these states have for technological rationality.

The new technocratic states are all engaged in rapid capitalistic development, and warmly welcome multinational corporations. To be attractive to foreign investment they must retain a political stability and a low wage structure. The first is achieved by repressing forms of dissent through control of popular movements of students, workers and peasants and by censorship of the flow of information. The security services and disciplinary bodies become increasingly sophisticated and pervasive. A strict control of the economy and the labour force enables a reservoir of low-salaried workers to be available. The irony of such states, as Kim Yong Bok describes it, is:

> Technocracy — the most rational way of doing things — creates historical consequences of physical violence, political violence and economic violence of the greatest magnitude. The people become objects of the technocracy, and victims of its violence.[7]

It is within these states with all their contradictions, that the people themselves must resolve their own forms of society. There will be many models from which to choose — democracy, Marxism, Maoism, socialism: the varieties of political development are all known and we are not here pleading for any particular one. But what we do seek as a moral imperative is the transformation of society so that structures and systems of injustice and domination give way to a new order in which human dignity is respected and basic human needs met.

The people know their political, economic and social leaders possess certain power and act according to a particular set of laws. But the people know that neither the power nor the laws are ultimate realities. There exists beyond these ephemeral phenomena a transcendental reality which is known by every person and which exists in that realm which holds the collective wisdom of humankind.

The people are not units to be manipulated for the benefit of "law and order" rulers, and they cannot be treated as battery hens. The people have their own dignity, and it is fundamental that the people should be seen as the subjects of history. It is not possible to speak of justice without a recognition of the participatory role of the people in the historic process.

If we take seriously, then, this assertion that the people are the subjects of history, then all our pressure for human rights is a way of giving sharper focus to the people's struggle to assert their own rights as humans and to restructure the existing power systems in order to let even the poor and the oppressed participate in their own society. As part of this massive struggle there will be many miniature battles. Each action of the people to secure their own rights or to express solidarity with others whose rights are being violated is another step towards affirming their essential dignity, and a part of the global struggle for justice.

The mission of the church

For Christians, the current human rights debate is a challenge to the integrity of the church. This becomes clear as we see the number of people who link human rights with the church's mission. "Human rights", says Emilio Castro of the WCC, "is not just the slogan of the political activist; it sums up the Christian missionary imperative."[8] A group of clergy meeting in Tiruvalla, South India, expressed the same thing antithetically: "The church's fear and inability to take a bold stance in the face of the violation of human rights amounts to a failure in mission."[9]

There is an ironic note of judgment running through these comments. The fact that it is necessary to persuade the church's hierarchy and members that human rights is the very text of the church's mission indicates how far the church has strayed from its identification with the people, and especially with the poor and the oppressed. A church which was identified with the dispossessed would not need these reminders. Unfortunately, we live with a curious ambivalence. The church has many times sought to preserve itself and to retain its own identity by removing itself from the scene of the people's struggle. This has led to many notable chapters of church history in which the faithful have accepted persecution and martyrdom rather than compromise with an injustice against the church. But the very emphasis on interiority and on the life of the church as an institution which this created, has turned the prayers and the witness of the people inward, and thus heightened the division which exists between those who live within the worshipping community of the institutional church and those who are outside.

The biblical witness is clear that the disjunction between the saved and the unsaved is not determined by membership in the institutional church, but by more basic issues of relationship to the people (Matt. 7 : 21; 25 : 44-46; Luke 9 : 49-50).

Consequently, any attempt on the part of the church either to abrogate to itself the decision about who is saved or who is not, or to stand apart from the people's suffering, is a failure to understand the meaning of salvation. The people do not exist to serve the church; they are subjects in their own right. And they are not to be treated as the object of mission, as has happened in foreign mission boards, and as still occurs in the missionary crusades "to build up the church". Nor are the people the objects of charity or of service projects. If we relate to the people as objects, we deny them their inalienable dignity which has been the gift of God to them, and which in conditions of extreme oppression is their last ontological reality. To strip the people of their dignity is to take away that which God has given.

The church should not stand apart from the people's legitimate struggles to be the subjects of history and the moulders of their own destiny. But this would place the church in an unaccustomed and threatening place. To stand in the place where the people are, will inexorably draw the church into opposition with ruling elites in oppressive nations. This has been the church's painful discovery in every continent in these past 20 years, and was illustrated in the case studies from three Asian countries. When the church accepts its obedience in mission it also accepts the scars which come from disobedience to the civil authorities.

Most human rights questions are extremely sensitive, and this means that the church must act with both discretion and sophistication; it must be wise as serpents and harmless as doves. What will this mean in praxis?

REPENTANCE AND HUMILITY

The basic stance of the church in approaching human rights questions will be one of repentance and humility. This is not an affected pose, but the painful recognition of the church's absence from many of the people's historic struggles for dignity. In a number of newly-independent countries it is the testimony of the people that the church stood with the forces of reaction when the people fought for their freedom. If today, in obedience to its mission, the church steps down from a position of elitism and privilege to share the people's struggle for their rights, it must be done in the self-emptying spirit — the kenosis — which was the mark of the ministry of Jesus.

WITNESS TO THE POWERFUL

In this spirit of humility, the church will be required to witness to the powerful that all systems, situations and authorities stand under the judgment of God. There is no perfectly just structure or power on the earth, and the church is one of the witnesses to remind both the rulers and the revolutionaries of this theological reality. At the same time, it must be made clear to authorities that the church's critical stance does not indicate disloyalty. It may be that this voice of witness will be the church's ultimate sign of loyalty to the state.

ATTACK ON THE ROOT CAUSES

The church will not just witness to the surface examples of human rights violations, but will be much more concerned to attack the root causes of these violations. In particular, there are three areas of social sin which demand this prophetic witness: (a) structures and systems which stifle freedom and impose various

64

forms of oppression on the people: these may be political, economic, militaristic, or ecclesiastical; *(b)* situations which promote
individual or group actions which dehumanize the people; *(c)* the
complicity of the people who stand apart from the situation and
who deny any responsibility for evil events.[10]

No second place

The church will assert that the rights of the people cannot take
second place to a national exigency. This is especially necessary
in the present historical moment, when rulers keep attempting to
deny the people their rights by creating fictions out of supposed
contradictions in society. The people are told you may have
human rights *or* economic development; human rights *or* national
security; bread *or* freedom. Against such false dichotomies the
church must assert that human rights cannot be subservient to any
earthly system. To divert the people from their dignity by offering
a false choice is too often a ploy to retain political power.

Identification with the people

Finally, the church will fulfill its mission as it stands for the
rights of the people to be the subjects of their own history. To
achieve this, the church must go to the people and be identified
with them. To say this is not to deify the people or to suggest
that their wisdom is beyond fault, but it is to recognize that in
the pain of the people, there is the pain of God; that in solidarity
with their suffering, there is the discovery of the risen Jesus.

A community of hope

Such a programme for the church requires new tools of analysis, and the development of flexible new instruments for opera-
tion within the actual situations of oppression. The events of
these past 20 years, in situations from Soweto to Chile, from
Harlem to Arnhem Land, and from Belfast to Seoul, have given
the international Christian community a range of experience in
standing with the oppressed people. In the process, the church
has made many mistakes, some more costly than others, but it
has also built up an international community of people whose
commitment to human rights is their obedience to Christ.

This emerging international community is grappling with new
questions about the life of the faith as it exists in oppressive situations. Among these new questions is the place of power in society,

especially in a burgeoning technocratic state. Since power begets power, the forms and sources of power available to the church must be examined. The biblical experience, especially that of the New Testament church, suggests that what is given to the church is the power to sustain community and keep its authenticity even when under attack. This was not a political or economic strength of the kind exhibited by the Roman Empire, but it was historically a permanent force. Today, the question is being asked in a different context, at a time when the principalities and powers have a strength which accentuates the weakness of the Christian community.

Another search is for authentic symbols of hope which speak the language of the people. In biblical times it was the symbol of exodus which sustained faith, and subsequent history has seen many national events which have provided the focus around which faith and hope could coalesce. What are the symbols for social imagination for the people today? What are the symbols which sustain the small Christian community under oppression, and are they capable of transformation to serve the wellbeing of the whole society? Modern Christian dialectics struggle with such questions, not only from an armchair, but also from the place of oppression.

It seems likely that the small, committed Christian community will be tested more and more by the dehumanizing forces at work in the world. Increasingly sophisticated methods of invasion of privacy, torture and technocratic control give increased power to the already powerful, and the so-called gross violations of human rights will become grosser. If these pressures continue, more people will be asking what Albert Camus claims is the ultimate question, "to decide whether life deserves to be lived or not".[11]

It is within the situation of suffering and oppression that the church must also stand as a community of hope: to affirm the basic dignity of the people and of each individual person; to work in this world for a new society based on the rights of the people; and to point towards the consummation of history as the sign of hope which makes the present struggle possible.

NOTES

1 Sean McBride, quoted by Niall MacDermot, QC, in a speech to the Canadian Human Rights Foundation, 21 November 1974 (mimeographed).

66

2 William Korey: "The UN's Double Standard on Human Rights." *Washington Post*, 22 May 1977, p. 13.

3 *Ibid.*, p. 13.

4 Ferdinand E. Marcos. *Newsweek*, 3 October 1977. His reference to the "Universal Declaration" should be to the Charter of the United Nations.

5 Jose Comblin: "The Church and the National Security System." *LADOC*, VI, 28, May-June 1976. Quoted under "Documentation" in *International Review of Mission*, WCC, Vol. LXVI, No. 263, July 1977, p. 265.

6 Herb Feith: "Techno-Fascism: a New Form of Tyranny?" Notes for politics department staff-graduate student seminar, 14 July 1976, Monash University, Australia (mimeographed).

7 Kim Yong Bok: "The People, Technocrats and Multi-national Corporations." *Towards a Theology of People*. Tokyo: CCA/URM, 1977, p. 105.

8 Emilio Castro: "Editorial." *International Review of Mission*, WCC, Vol. LXVI, No. 263, July 1977, p. 216.

9 *Religion and Society*, CISRS, June and September 1977, p. 68.

10 Summary of the Second Roman Synod: "Justice in the World", November 1971. In "The Concept of Social Sin", Peter J. Henriot SJ, October 1973 (mimeographed).

11 Quoted in Gustavo Gutierrez: *Theology of Liberation*. London: SCM, 1974, p. 50.

Appendices

APPENDIX I
SOME BIBLICAL CONSIDERATIONS

At one level, the Bible is an historical record of the struggle of a small section of humanity to create a nation. It is the chronology of Israel's progression from being a nomadic people to a more settled form of agriculture and the establishment of urban centres. Within this process, the Bible records revolutions and changes in political systems; it gives chronicles and economic indicators; biographies of kings, prostitutes and holy men, as well as poetry, songs and folk history.

But the unique quality of the Bible is not in its record of secular events, but the fact that it sees this secular procession of history as the human search for God. The writers had a type of early historical determinism in which secular events were interpreted from a religious viewpoint and thereby given a theological quality. They were supremely confident — even to the point of arrogance — that Israel had a special place in the Plan of God, and thus even the mini-events of history had a pregnant significance as part of the wider movement of the chosen people of God.

Within this secular-religious context, Israel evolved some germinal concepts of human behaviour which have become significant for our contemporary understanding of human rights. The strength of this long Judeo-Christian tradition can be seen reflected in the major declarations of modern states, and particularly in the constitutional declarations of the United States of America and France and the United Nations "Universal Declaration of Human Rights". Of more immediate consequence is the fact that those persons whose rights have been violated have, in many cases, found strength for their resistance in the text of biblical symbolism.

The inimitable human

In Jewish folk history man was not just another created species like a chicken or a fish; man was the final act of creation, the unique and inimitable creature who occupied a special place in the eyes of a munificent creator.

> Yet you have made him little less than a god,
> you have crowned him with glory and splendour,
> and made him lord over the work of your hands,
> set all things under his feet. (Ps. 8 : 5-6)

The phrase which best captures this human uniqueness is in the account of creation. In the priestly code of Genesis the creation is described as the result of God's self-deliberation:

Let us make man in our own image (selem 'eĺohīm)
in the likeness of ourselves. (Gen. 1 : 26a)

It is this act of grace at the moment of creation which endows each person with a unique and intrinsically intimate relationship with the creator. By this action God gives to all people the particularism of human dignity which determines their responsibility both towards himself and the totality of his creation. Their rights as human persons are derivative from the fundamental affirmation that at their genesis they were created in the image of God (*imago dei*).

What does it mean for the people to affirm that they are the image of God? Theologians have given many answers to this question, and a full listing of the proposals reads like a thesaurus of abstract nouns of personality.[1] More recently, exegesis of the text has concentrated on the fact that the plural form is used for man (*adam*) and for God (*'eĺohīm*). The use of the collective noun can be understood in the next verse:

God created man in the image of himself,
in the image of God he created him,
male and female he created them. (Gen. 1 : 27)

Verse 27b is said by Karl Barth to be the "definitive explanation" to the meaning of the *imago dei*.[2] Just as the triune God is not alone within himself, so he creates people to be together and to complement themselves in love. They are the image of God in their covenantal relationship, and it is in this possibility and capacity for covenantal relationship that their uniqueness inheres. Image is, therefore, not a thing which the people have as an automatic endowment. It is a hope and a promise. The divine likeness is found only in its perfect state in Jesus Christ, and is imparted through him. As persons enter into the covenantal relationship with Christ so they are in the image of God. Only through such a conditional interpretation can we make sense of our human condition.

The relationship must be qualified. It is a covenant relationship which is the essence of God's image. Within such a relationship the people have the possibility to become fully human and fulfil their creator's promise of being made in his likeness. It is this act of grace at the moment of creation which gives to all people their inherent worth, and which must be the starting point for Christian affirmations on human rights. Pope Pius XII affirms that "the dignity of man is the dignity of the image of God".[3] It is this unique nature of the human that makes the Christian conscience protest against any attitude, word or action which treats the people as objects, as things, to be manipulated. The impersonal or oppressive society thus becomes not only an attack on the dignity of man but also a sin against God.

Liberation from oppression

The story of creation was written after the events of the Exodus. This historical experience of liberation from oppression clarified the Israelite view of humanity. It accelerated the transition of a nomadic, wilderness people into a more settled nation and became the watershed for Israel's religious and historic experience.

> "I brought you out of the
>   land of Egypt:
> You alone of all the families
>   of earth,
> have I acknowledged." (Amos 3 : 1-2)

The Exodus was the formative event for Israel's religious thought. It confirmed their relationship with God, because when they were under the oppressive system of Egypt, "God heard their groaning ... God looked down upon the sons of Israel and he knew..." (Ex. 2 : 24-25). This was the salvic history of the nation.

The symbols of Exodus have been woven into the history and experiences of countless other subsequent societies, and they have provided the metaphors for many struggles of oppressed people in oppressive situations. In a present-day prison cell in Korea, the poet Kim Chi Ha draws inspiration from the imagery of the Exodus.

> Only when the people struggle out of the darkness, driven along by the very chaos of their opposition to authority, will they reach the sun-drenched fields. Then they can head towards Canaan, the land of justice and freedom promised by the Creator. This is my dream, my faith. I cannot describe Canaan in detail. No one man can do that. I think it will be created by the collective effort of all the people. My task is to fight on until the people hold the power in their own hands to shape their destiny.[4]

So it has happened that the determination of a small group of nomadic people to be free from oppression has passed into the folk history of other cultures influenced by the Judeo-Christian civilization. The Exodus event became one of the great formative stories of history. Through it the Israelite people had stood up. No longer were they the slaves and servants who endured flogging and abuse with a demeaning obsequiousness. The people had regained their essential dignity. This deliverance set the framework for the biblical understanding of history. But as with many successful liberation struggles, time gave it an unreal triumphalism and the people developed an over-optimistic view of their destiny. Not many generations passed before the people were consistently rejecting the idealism which was produced in the euphoria of this "nationalist" victory.

Prophetic witness

For three hundred years after the Exodus, Israel kept its unity and codified its traditional patterns of behaviour into law.[5] From such foundations evolved the concern for righteousness (Saddik) and justice (mishpāt) which was the ideal to be sought in the structure of society (Deut. 16 : 20).

After the death of King Solomon in 931 B.C. the kingdom divided and history entered a new and turbulent era. During this time a group of strong-willed individuals emerged with the special function of recalling the people to a way of life based on the Sinai covenant. The voice of the prophet was heard in the land.

The Old Testament prophets were unacceptable persons. To political authorities and commercial capitalists, they represented a subversive threat to stability. It is the nature of those who benefit from a system to keep the system immutable and thus preserve their privilege, so they made sure that the words of indignation from the prophets fell on deaf ears. The ruling class used smear tactics and, where necessary, force to denigrate the prophetic call. The prophets were ridiculed as the "troublers of Israel" (I Kings 18 : 17). Jeremiah barely escaped the death penalty, Daniel was placed in a den of lions, and others suffered indignities at the hands of the rulers and the people. Loneliness and rejection are the fate of the person driven by conviction to make a prophetic witness against the principalities and powers of the status quo.

When the prophets spoke of violence, they consistently linked this word with oppression.[6]

> You (the king)... have eyes and heart for nothing
> but your own interests,

> for shedding innocent blood
> and perpetrating violence and oppression. (Jer. 22 : 17)

Micah says the same about the rich man (Micah 6 : 12) and
Ezekiel about the princes (Ezek. 45 : 9). It has been customary
in recent history to link violence with minorities and revolutionary
groups within society, but the prophets do not think in these
terms. For them, the roots of violence always lie with those
who possess power and who, in their power, have chosen to
disregard the nation's covenantal heritage. When political and
economic power is used to oppress the people, society moves
invariably to violence.

However, the prophets were not advocating an alternative
political or economic ideology. The tradition which had been
handed down from Moses had divine ratification and their call
was, therefore, to return to this covenant and observe it. Within
the proximate historical event, they advocated no political
alternative but, rather, a renewal of the just society which God
had called Israel to become. The prophets had a clear conviction
about God's judgment on those who exploited the poor (Amos 8 :
4-6; Jer. 6 : 27-30; Micah 2 : 1-3). Yahweh would surely punish
those who practise injustice. The prophets add a new moral
dimension to Israel's understanding of the poor by asserting that
there is no necessary connection between righteousness and
prosperity, since the experience during the monarchies showed
that "wealth generated power through which the poor were
robbed of their rights".[7] The presence of this poverty brought
God's judgment on the whole society. Bonino says:

> To the prophet poverty is not a hazard of fortune or a fact of
> nature but the result of certain people's greed and injustice. It is
> intolerable because it contradicts the very purpose of God's mighty
> act of deliverance — to rescue his people from the slavery of Egypt.[8]

When it came to these poor, the prophets had no doubt about
God's word.

> Woe to the legislators of infamous laws,
> To those who issue tyrannical decrees,
> Who refuse justice to the unfortunate
> And cheat the poor among my people of their rights. (Isa. 10 : 1-2)

The prophets lend strong support to Karl Barth's affirmation
that "God always takes his stand unconditionally and passionately
on this side and this side alone: against the lofty and in behalf
of the lowly".[9]

Jesus — the Messiah who suffers

A new covenant begins with the coming of Jesus. In him, the promise inherent in creation, the hope of liberation prefigured in the Exodus and the word of the prophets are all made flesh.[10] That is, they are all expressed in a concrete form which is intelligible within human history. Jesus exegetes the history of the people.

Where does Jesus stand or, more correctly, with whom does he stand? Who are the people for whom God enters history? At one level he is indiscriminate. No person is excluded on grounds of class or station. Jesus has friends among the rulers (Nicomedus [11]) as well as with the ordinary citizens; He speaks with the rich (the young ruler [12]), and with the poor (the widow [13]); He has dealings with the pillars of society (Zacheus [14]), and with the revolutionaries (Simon Zealot [15]). His friends are from all strata of society. Yet there is a distinction in his teaching. To the rich he gives the challenge of the poor (Zacheus and the young ruler) and to the powerful he speaks of the frailty of power (Nicodemus). The inference of these encounters is that Jesus stands primarily for the oppressed and those who are the victims of society.

To say that Jesus stands on the side of the poor has become something of a cliché in modern ecumenical discussion. It is true that in the gospels, whenever a choice is required Jesus stands with the poor, but this cannot be universally applied to romanticize the position of the poor. Nor should it be implied that Jesus has favourites and selects one category of people by category alone.

It is better to affirm that Jesus is on the side of the human. It is in the poor and the oppressed that we are forced to face the meaning of human existence, and his stand with the poor becomes an affirmation of those human relations by which we become fully free and completely human.

This is a far cry from the idealization of the poor. The poor have their own wisdom, but whenever the situation changes and the poor become rich they are just as oppressive as their former masters. The experience of poverty is no immunization against later living a sinful and oppressive life. This is the core of the parable of the unforgiving debtor which Jesus taught (Matt. 18: 23-25).

In Galilee he begins his ministry with a sermon based on justice. His vocation is said to include the bringing of good news to the poor, and the proclamation of liberty to the captives, and the setting free of the downtrodden (Luke 4 : 18, 19). He comes as one of the poor (II Cor. 8 : 9) and teaches us through this example "to look on the poor as the extension of his own presence among us".[16]

The dignity and worth of the people is a continuing theme of Jesus. They are so important to God that the hairs on their head are numbered,[17] and this is true for both good and bad alike.[18] People come before institutions or religious ceremony.[19] The criterion by which our actions must be judged is the way in which we have upheld the dignity of the people.

The incarnation is, therefore, an affirmation of people's dignity. The *imago dei* of creation is reinterpreted and is placed within the grasp of all people as they share in a new covenantal relationship with Christ. In him a new day begins for humanity. "Yes, God loved the world so much" (John 3 : 16a) is the highest evidence of Godly concern for mankind that can be expressed. In Jesus the Messiah, God is saying "yes" to humanity. It is a "yes" to the inherent and inalienable rights and dignity of the people, and a "yes" to the working out of God's reality in the earthy, secular, daily history of the people. With all of its oppression, its denial of human rights, its attacks on human dignity, its sham and drudgery, ridicule, hatred and evil, it is still the world to which God has said "yes" in Jesus Christ.

The breadth of God's "yes" does not stop with the incarnation. It becomes purified and perfected in Jesus' death. In the final suffering and crucifixion, Jesus the Messiah becomes Jesus the Victim. In permitting and, by his own freedom, accepting the victimization, Jesus becomes the man for others. For it is the victim and not the oppressor who speaks to us of our humanity. It is through the weakness of the suffering one that the people are permitted the glimpse of the eternal. And it is in sharing his suffering that we are healed (Phil. 3 : 10).

The actual historical Jesus remains a shadowy figure, unknown to us except through the writings of a few of his followers. His words have been overlaid by centuries of tradition, interpretation, translation and superstition. Each person's typification of Jesus will, therefore, draw on a whole range of previous experiences and be heavily conditioned by the situation from which the person is looking. The ragged poor in the slums of Calcutta will see a different Jesus from the one worshipped by the wealthy tycoons of Houston, Texas. To the people who are the victims of human rights violations, the suffering victim is the sustaining typification of Jesus. "Nobody knows the trouble I've seen," says the Negro spiritual, "nobody knows but Jesus." Across all generations and to all types of afflicted people, the suffering Jesus speaks in a voice they can understand.

An aborigine woman endeavouring to explain the suffering of her people wrote a memorandum to Jesus Christ to explain her troubles.[20] In South Asia, I once spoke with a young Asian Christian who had been tortured for several days but was able to survive it more successfully than any of his companions. When asked what had given him the strength, he told of a painting of the crucifixion in his mother's room and explained that he had held this picture in his mind the whole time with the belief that if Christ had suffered, his disciple could also.

The life and the suffering of Jesus have become a powerful symbol for the oppressed. To Asian Christians he is the paradigm to whom they look in oppression, and whose call is to be obeyed. "We are commanded by our Lord Jesus Christ to live among the oppressed, the poor and the despised *as he did* in Judea." [21] Through his incarnation and victimization all suffering people find their redemption and their hope.

Human destiny

Central to Christian teaching is the belief that history has a direction. God is working his purpose out in the experiences of the people, and all things are moving towards that great consummation when the new heaven and the new earth appear and there is no more injustice among the people (Rev. 21 : 1-4). It is this enormous sense of historic importance which gives Christian believers the power to sustain any kind of persecution or ridicule, because they believe that no matter how others may see it, their life has meaning and purpose. No higher recognition can be accorded to human dignity.

The sharpness of this historical sense can be seen in the writings of the Korean patriot Kim San who claims:

A man's name and his brief dream may be buried with his bones, but nothing that he has ever done or failed to do is lost in the final balance of forces... Nothing can rob a man of his place in the

> movement of history. His only individual decision is whether to move forward or backward, whether to fight or submit, whether to create value or destroy it, whether to be strong or weak.[22]

The contrast between the great heavenly kingdom of the future and the misery and oppression under which many people live in the present, has encouraged some sects of Christianity to renounce the present world altogether. This is not a biblical concept. The vision of the future is not meant to make people despair of the present, but rather to persuade them to act for change. The heavenly kingdom of the future is a prototype for contemporary action.

This is made clear in the parable of the last judgment in Matthew 25 : 31-46. The cosmic purpose of God is realized by very ordinary and mundane acts of community which show compassion for the casualties of society. The suffering of others is not to be avoided but to be embraced by identity with the people and taking some action, however simple, to serve the people who are in distress. It is in feeding the hungry, visiting the prisoners and clothing the ragged that the requirements of God are fulfilled. It is an extraordinary paradox that the "last" judgment is our present action.

The ultimate goal of human destiny which the Bible places before us prevents idealism about the contemporary struggle. Revolutionaries often speak and act as if the immediate goal is the ultimate goal. They will infer that the death of a dictator, or the overthrow of a colonial power or the ouster of a government will usher in utopia. This is not true to history or to biblical theology. There is much human sin in all living history and the revolution is often betrayed first by its own leadership.

The antidote to reading history with despair is the conviction that human destiny lies in the hands of God. As the people work for human community, human dignity and human rights they share in what the Bible calls the *arabon* (the promise or the down-payment) of the kingdom. It is within this struggle for a just human political, economic and social system on earth that the people find their own humanity.

It is from such biblical affirmations that we recognize the need to work for the rights and the dignity of the people. "Yes, God loved the world so much" (John 3 : 16).

76

NOTES

1 Modern Catholic writings favour "intelligence, will... and the moral sense which moves him (man) to act according to laws laid down by the creator". Pontifical commission "Justicia et Pax": *The Church and Human Rights*. Vatican City, 1975, p. 32 — "Knowledge" is proposed by A. Kuyper in G. Berkouwer: *Man: the Image of God*. Grands Rapids, Mich.: Eerdmans, 1962, p. 39, and James Orr suggests "spiritual, self-conscious being, rationality, capacity for moral life" in Berkouwer, *ibid.*, p. 39 — The image is defined as "rational structure" by Paul Tillich: *Systematic Theology*. Chicago: University of Chicago, 1957, Vol. II, p. 49 — A summary by William Horden: "Man, Doctrine of". In *A Dictionary of Christian Theology*, ed. A. Richardson. London: SCM, 1969, pp. 202-204, and R. Niebuhr: *The Nature and Destiny of Man*. New York: Scribners, 1949, pp. 150-166.

2 Karl Barth: *Church Dogmatics*. Edinburgh: T. & T. Clark, 1958, III, Vol. 1, p. 183 f.

3 Pope Pius XII: "Christmas Broadcast, 1944." In *The Church and Human Rights*, *op. cit.*, p. 29.

4 Kim Chi Ha: "Declaration of Conscience", trans. by the Committee to Rescue Kim Chi Ha and His Friends. In T. K.: *Letters from South Korea*. Tokyo: Iwanami Shoten, 1976, p. 394.

5 Found in the Code of the Covenant (Ex. 20 : 22-23 : 19), the Deuteronomic Code (Deut. 12-26) and the Code of Holiness (Lev. 17-26).

6 Herman Hendrickx: *The Bible on Justice*. Manila, no publisher, 1975, p. 4.

7 L. E. Keck: "Poor." In *The Interpreter's Dictionary of the Bible*. Nashville, Tenn.: Abingdon, 1976, supplementary volume, pp. 672-673.

8 José Miguez Bonino: *Revolutionary Theology Comes of Age*. London: SPCK, 1975, p. 112.

9 Karl Barth, *op. cit.*, II, Vol. 1, p. 386.

10 *Jerusalem Bible*. Footnote John 1.

11 John 3 : 1-21.

12 Mark 10 : 17-22.

13 Mark 12 : 41-44.

14 Luke 19 : 1-10.

15 Luke 6 : 15.

16 Herman Hendrickx, *op. cit.*, p. 103.

17 Matt. 10 : 30.

18 Matt. 5 : 45.

19 Matt. 9 : 10-13, 5 : 23-29.

20 Maureen Watson: "Memo to J.C." In Ron O'Grady and Lee Soo Jin, eds: *Suffering and Hope*. Singapore: CCA, 1976, p. 43.

21 "Theological Declaration of Korean Christians, 1973." In *Documents on the Struggle for Democracy in Korea*. Tokyo: Shinkyo Shuppansha, 1975, p. 39.

22 Kim San: "Epilogue." In O'Grady and Lee, *op. cit.*, p. 79.

APPENDIX II
SELECTED BIBLIOGRAPHY

A listing of some of the source material for current ethical concerns for human rights.

A. General works

BENN, STANLEY I.: "Human Rights." *The Encyclopaedia of Philosophy*. New York: Macmillan, 1967, Vol. VII.

DE CHARDIN, TEILHARD: *The Future of Man*. Fontana Books. London: Collins, 1974.

CRANSTON, MAURICE: *What Are Human Rights?* London: Bodley Head, 1973.

KISSINGER, HENRY A.: "Morality and Power." The role of human rights in foreign policy, *The Guardian*, Manchester, UK, October 9, 1977.

KOREY, WILLIAM: "The UN's Double Standard on Human Rights." *Washington Post*, May 22, 1977.

McGREGOR, IAN: *Human Rights*. World-Wide Series. London: Batsford, 1975.

SCHLESINGER, ARTHUR, JR.: "Human Rights, How Far, How Fast?" *Asian Wall Street Journal*, March 8, 1977.

SCHWELB, EGON: "Human Rights." In *Encyclopaedia Britannica*, 15th ed., 1975, Macropaedia 8.

VANCE, CYRUS J.: "Speech to University of Georgia." *Washington Post*, May 1, 1977 and *The Guardian*, Manchester, UK, May 8, 1977.

B. Historical background

1. GENERAL

FRENCH NATIONAL ASSEMBLY: *Declaration of the Rights of Man and of Citizens*. Paris, August 1789.

LOCKE, JOHN: *Essay Concerning Civil Government*. 1690.

MARX, KARL and ENGELS, FRIEDRICH: *Marx and Engels, Basic Writings*, ed. Lewis S. Feuer. Fontana Classics. London: Collins, 1974.

MILL, JOHN STUART: *Essay on Liberty*. The Pelican Classics. Aylesbury: Penguin, 1976.

UNITED NATIONS GENERAL ASSEMBLY: "Universal Declaration of Human Rights." December 10, 1948.

UNITED NATIONS GENERAL ASSEMBLY: "Covenant on Economic, Social and Cultural Rights." December 16, 1966.

UNITED NATIONS GENERAL ASSEMBLY: "Covenant on Civil and Political Rights." December 16, 1966.

UNITED NATIONS GENERAL ASSEMBLY: "Optional Protocol to the Covenant on Civil and Political Rights." December 16, 1966.

UNITED NATIONS, GENERAL ASSEMBLY: "The United Nations and Human Rights." Office of Public Information. New York: UN, 1973.

UNITED STATES CONGRESS: *Bill of Rights*. September 25, 1789.

2. CHURCHES

CHRISTIAN CONFERENCE OF ASIA: *Statement on Human Rights*. Hong Kong, August 30, 1974.

CHRISTIAN CONFERENCE OF ASIA: *Human Rights in Asia*. General Committee resolution. Singapore, March 4-8, 1975.

COMMISSION OF THE CHURCHES ON INTERNATIONAL AFFAIRS, World Council of Churches: *The Churches in International Affairs*. Reports 1970-1973. Geneva: WCC, 1974, pp. 69-139.

COMMISSION OF THE CHURCHES ON INTERNATIONAL AFFAIRS, World Council of Churches: *Human Rights and Christian Responsibility*, 3 Vols. Geneva: WCC, 1974, mimeographed.

MACDERMOT, NIALL, QC: *Human Rights and the Churches*. Speech to Catholic Institute for International Relations. London, June 15, 1976.

NOLDE, O. FREDERICK: *Free and Equal*. Geneva: WCC, 1968.

VAN DEN HEUVEL, ALBERT: "The Churches and Human Rights." *Mid-Stream*, Council on Christian Unity of the Christian Church (Disciples of Christ), Indianapolis, USA, April 1977, pp. 218-228.

WORLD COUNCIL OF CHURCHES: *The Ten Formative Years 1938-1948*. Geneva, 1948, pp. 57, 58.

WORLD COUNCIL OF CHURCHES: *The First Six Years 1948-1954*. Geneva, 1954, pp. 97-98.

WORLD COUNCIL OF CHURCHES: *Evanston to New Delhi*. Geneva, 1961, pp. 135-138.

WORLD COUNCIL OF CHURCHES: *The New Delhi Report*. London: SCM Press, 1961.

WORLD COUNCIL OF CHURCHES: *The Uppsala Report*, ed. Norman Goodall. Geneva, 1968, pp. 63, 64, 144-148, 186, 187.

WORLD COUNCIL OF CHURCHES: *Uppsala to Nairobi*, ed. David Johnson. London: SPCK, and Grand Rapids: Eerdmans, 1975, pp. 134-136.

WORLD COUNCIL OF CHURCHES: *Breaking Barriers: Nairobi, 1975*, ed. David M. Paton. London: SPCK, and Grand Rapids: Eerdmans, 1976, pp. 102-119, 169-180.

C. Theological background

1. GENERAL WORKS

BARTH, KARL: *Church Dogmatics*, trans. J. W. Edwards, O. Bussey and Harold Knight. Edinburgh: T. & T. Clark, 1958, Vol. 1, p. 183 f, Vol. 2, p. 508 f.

BERKOUWER, G. C.: *Man: the Image of God*. Grand Rapids: Eerdmans, 1962.

BONHOEFFER, DIETRICH: *Letters and Papers from Prison*. London: SCM, 1954.

BONINO, JOSE MIGUEZ, ed.: *Revolutionary Theology Comes of Age*. London: SPCK, 1975.

BUBER, MARTIN: *Between Man and Man*, trans. R. G. Smith. London: Fontana, 1974.

CHRISTIAN CONFERENCE OF ASIA/URM: *Towards a Theology of People*. Tokyo: CCA, 1977.

GUTIERREZ, GUSTAVO: *A Theology of Liberation*, trans. Caridad Inda and John Eagleson. New York: Orbis, 1975.

HENDRICKX, HERMAN: *The Bible on Justice*. Manila: no publisher, 1975.

HOUTART, FRANCOIS and ROUSSEAU, ANDRÉ: *The Church and Revolution*, trans. Violet Nevile. New York: Orbis, 1971.

KEE, ALISTAIR: *A Reader in Political Theology*. London: SCM, 1974.

NIEBUHR, R.: *The Nature and Destiny of Man*. New York: Scribners, 1949, pp. 150-166.

TILLICH, PAUL: *Systematic Theology*. University of Chicago, 1957, Vol. II, p. 49 f.

2. HUMAN RIGHTS

BONINO, JOSE MIGUEZ: "Whose Human Rights?" *International Review of Mission*, WCC, Vol. LXVI, No. 263, July 1977, pp. 220-224.

FRENZ, HELMUT: "Human Rights, a Christian Viewpoint." *Christianity and Crisis*, New York, June 21, 1976, pp. 146-151.

JENKINS, DAVID: "Human Rights in Christian Perspective." *Study Encounter*, WCC, No. 2, 1974.

JUSTICIA ET PAX, PONTIFICAL COMMISSION: *The Church and Human Rights*. Maurice, Cardinal Roy, President, Vatican City, 1974.

WORLD ALLIANCE OF REFORMED CHURCHES: *Theological Basis of Human Rights*. Geneva: WARC, 1976.

WORLD COUNCIL OF CHURCHES: *The Ecumenical Review*, issue on human rights, WCC, Vol. XXVII, No. 2, 1975.

D. Human rights in Asia

1. GENERAL WORKS

ANDERSON, GERALD H.: *Asian Voices in Christian Theology*. New York: Orbis, 1976.

CAMERON, NIGEL: *From Bondage to Liberation: East Asia 1860-1952*. Hong Kong: Oxford University Press, 1975.

ELWOOD, DOUGLAS J.: *What Asian Christians are Thinking*. Manila: New Day, 1976.

FITZGERALD, C. P.: *History of East Asia*. Harmondsworth, UK: Penguin, 1974.

KIM, YONG BOK: "Reflections on People's Rights in Asia." Paper presented to Asia Youth Mission, Lantau Island, Hong Kong, May 1977.

KRIANGSAK, CHAMANAND GENERAL: "What Price Human Rights?" *Far Eastern Economic Review*, Hong Kong, July 22, 1977.

LEE, KWAN YEW: *Straits Times*, Singapore, May 6, 1977.

LIN, YUTANG: *The Wisdom of China and India*. Taipei: Literature House, 1968.

O'GRADY, RON and LEE, SOO JIN: *Suffering and Hope*. Singapore: CCA, 1976.

Report of Seminar on Religion and Development in Asian Societies. Colombo, Sri Lanka: Marga, 1974.

2. PEOPLE'S REPUBLIC OF CHINA

MACINNIS, DONALD E.: *Religious Policy and Practice in Communist China*. New York: Macmillan, 1972.

NATIONAL COUNCIL OF THE CHURCHES OF CHRIST IN THE USA: *Documents of the Three-Self Movement*. New York: NCCC, 1963.

WHITEHEAD, RHEA: "China and the Churches in the Struggle for Human Rights." *China Notes*, New York, Fall, 1976.

3. INDIA

CHRISTIAN INSTITUTE FOR THE STUDY OF RELIGION AND SOCIETY: "The Crisis of Democracy and the Implementation of the 20-Point Programme." *Religion and Society*, Bangalore, June 1976.

CHRISTIAN INSTITUTE FOR THE STUDY OF RELIGION AND SOCIETY: "Christians and the Emergency: Some Documents." *Religion and Society*, Bangalore, Vol. XXII, Nos 2 and 3, June and September 1977.

DEVANESEN, CHANDRAN D. S. and ABEL, M.: "The Powers of Government and the Claims of Human Freedom." In *Responsible Government in a Revolutionary Age*, ed. Z. K. Mathews. New York: Association Press, 1976, pp. 183-196.

KURIEN, C. T.: "Indian Elections: an Interpretation." Madras, 1977, mimeographed.

NAYAR, KULDIP: *The Judgment*. New Delhi: Vikas, 1977.

4. REPUBLIC OF KOREA

EMERGENCY CHRISTIAN CONFERENCE ON KOREAN PROBLEMS: *Documents on the Struggle for Democracy in Korea*. Tokyo: Shinkyo Shuppansha, 1975.

JAPAN EMERGENCY CHRISTIAN CONFERENCE ON KOREAN PROBLEMS: *Korea Communique*, chairman John Nakajima. Monthly since August 1946.

JAPANESE CATHOLIC COUNCIL FOR JUSTICE AND PEACE: "Report from the Trial of Kim Chi Ha." Tokyo, 1976, mimeographed.

KIM, CHI HA: *Cry of the People and Other Poems*. Kanagawa-ken, Japan: Autumn Press, 1974.

KIM, CHI HA: "Declaration of Conscience from Prison." *AMPO*, the Japan-Asia Quarterly Review, Tokyo, July-September, 1975, pp. 36-49. Alternative translation in T.K.: *Letters from South Korea*, pp. 389-408.

KIM, DAE JUNG: "Some Day We Will be Free." *Newsweek*, November 22, 1976, p. 11.

KIM, KWAN SUK: "We Want Moral Support." *Newsweek*, May 30, 1977, p. 19.

"South Korea Under Emergency Rule." *Pro Mundi Vita Dossiers*, Brussels, January 1976.

T.K.: *Letters from South Korea*, trans. David L. Swain. Tokyo: Iwanami Shoten, 1976.

5. REPUBLIC OF THE PHILIPPINES

A Message of Hope to Filipinos Who Care. Manila: KKK, 1975.

AMNESTY INTERNATIONAL: *Report of Mission to the Philippines*. London: AI, 1976.

ASSOCIATION OF MAJOR RELIGIOUS SUPERIORS IN THE PHILIPPINES: *Political Detainees in the Philippines*. Manila: AMRSP, 1976. Revised 1977.

ASSOCIATION OF MAJOR RELIGIOUS SUPERIORS IN THE PHILIPPINES: *Signs of the Times*. January to April, 1976.

CLAVER, FRANCISCO F. and SALONGA, JOVITO R.: *Faith and Justice and the Filipino Christian*. Alay Kapwa Lectures. Manila: LST, 1976.

DEL ROSARIO S. G.: *The Church and State Today*. Quezon City: Manlapaz, 1975.

INTERNATIONAL COMMISSION OF JURISTS: *The Decline of Democracy in the Philippines*. A report of missions by William J. Butler, John P. Humphrey and G. E. Bisson. Geneva: ICJ, 1977.

MARCOS, FERDINAND E.: *The Democratic Revolution in the Philippines*. New Jersey: Prentice Hall, 1974.

MARCOS, FERDINAND E.: "Interview." *Newsweek*, October 3, 1977, pp. 7-8.